SIGNS, SUPERSTITIONS, AND GOD'S PLAN

SIGNS, SUPERSTITIONS, AND GOD'S PLAN

THE HUMAN QUEST FOR MEANING

Brian Schmisek

Paulist Press
New York / Mahwah, NJ

Cover design by Joe Gallagher
Book design by Lynn Else

Library of Congress Cataloging-in-Publication Data
Names: Schmisek, Brian, author.
Title: Signs, superstitions, and God's plan : the human quest for meaning / Brian Schmisek.
Description: New York / Mahwah, NJ : Paulist Press, [2022] | Includes index. | Summary: "An examination of the various ways human beings make sense and meaning of the world, concluding with a call to personal agency"—Provided by publisher.
Identifiers: LCCN 2021062743 (print) | LCCN 2021062744 (ebook) | ISBN 9780809156153 (paperback) | ISBN 9780809187768 (ebook)
Subjects: LCSH: Meaning (Philosophy) | Meaning (Philosophy)—Religious aspects—Christianity.
Classification: LCC B105.M4 S36 2022 (print) | LCC B105.M4 (ebook) | DDC 121/.68—dc23/eng/20220218
LC record available at https://lccn.loc.gov/2021062743
LC ebook record available at https://lccn.loc.gov/2021062744

ISBN 978-0-8091-5615-3 (paperback)
ISBN 978-0-8091-8776-8 (e-book)

Published by Paulist Press
997 Macarthur Boulevard
Mahwah, New Jersey 07430
www.paulistpress.com

Printed and bound in the
United States of America

CONTENTS

FOREWORD

by John L. Allen Jr.

As I write these lines, a massive Russian invasion of Ukraine is underway, triggering fears of a wider European conflict. Television screens all around the world are occupied nearly 24/7 by ex-military figures, diplomats, and pundits, all opining on the wider geopolitical significance of what's unfolding before our eyes. Is President Vladimir Putin attempting to reconstruct the old Soviet Empire? Is there any truth to claims that the ethnically Russian population of eastern Ukraine has been mistreated, and that their aspirations for autonomy are legitimate? Will this crisis mark a defining moment for NATO, or will the alliance be revealed to be largely feckless in the face of naked aggression? Will the Ukraine crisis rescue the Biden presidency, allowing him to demonstrate strong leadership under fire, or will it be the final nail in the coffin?

In other circles, however, a different sort of analysis is going on. Pastor Tim Johnson of Countryside Baptist Church in Parke County, Indiana, posted an item on his "Preacher's Point" blog analyzing the Russian offensive in terms of the prophecy of Ezekiel 38—39, which describes a terrible battle involving Gog of Magog (identified by Johnson with Russia) that eventually involves Israel and the Arab states surrounding it. All of this, as Johnson sees it, suggests that biblical prophecies about the end times are playing out. Gerald Flurry, pastor general of the Philadelphia Church of God and host of the

"Key of David" television program, agreed that Ezekiel 38 was key, publishing a piece in which he cited verse 1: "Mortal, set your face toward Gog, of the land of Magog, the chief prince of Meshech and Tubal. Prophesy against him," and identified Putin as the "chief prince" in the verse. "Prophecy is proving to be right again and again!" Flurry wrote. "When will we stop and listen to what God prophesies? Until we do, the wars will only continue!"

If a Tim Johnson or a Gerald Flurry were to somehow drop in on one of the hard-nosed policy panels we're seeing on the CNNs and BBCs of the world, they would likely be laughed off the air, dismissed as religious zealots interpreting current events through the lens of an enigmatic ancient book rather than *Realpolitik*. Yet the truth of the matter is that far more people around the world today are inclined to think in the spiritual and supernatural categories invoked by the two pastors than the Harvard School of Government filters of the pundits. Almost 30 percent of Americans report that they have witnessed divine healings, for example, according to a Pew Research Center study, while 56 percent of Guatemalans, 71 percent of Kenyans, 62 percent of Nigerians, and 44 percent of Indians claim to have done so. Roughly 11 percent of Americans claim to have experienced or witnessed exorcisms, while 34 percent of Brazilians, 38 percent of Guatemalans, 61 percent of Kenyans, 57 percent of Nigerians, and 28 percent of Filipinos say they have had these experiences.

As David Brooks once put it of the elite pundit class dominating our airwaves today, "A great Niagara of religious fervor is cascading down around them, while they stand obtuse and dry in the little cave of their own parochialism."

My professional experience of almost twenty-five years certainly confirms the point. I'm a journalist covering the Vatican and the papacy, and I've travelled all over the world reporting Catholic stories from the pope to ordinary rank-and-file believers. While it's certainly possible to cover the Vatican entirely on the basis of politics and organizational dynamics, ignoring the spiritual dimension of why it does what it does, and how people react to it, is a surefire prescription for missing something important. The same could be said for virtually any other story a reporter might ever cover, from the COVID-19 pandemic to rising oil prices. If you don't appreciate that lots of people are going to think about those things in terms of supernatural forces, you're choosing to be deliberately indifferent to reality—which, ironically enough, is a charge that secularists usually level at believers, but of which they're often as guilty as anyone else.

Fortunately, we now have Brian Schmisek's *Signs, Superstitions, and God's Plan* as a corrective. Drawing on sources who range from Cicero and Josephus to Viktor Frankl and E. O. Wilson, Schmisek surveys how the desire to find a deeper meaning to seemingly random events is a constant in human experience, from antiquity to five minutes ago. He provides a useful set of categories for analyzing the way people go about it, opening up the thought world of seeing current events through the lens of prophecy, divine causation, and "signs and wonders." Toward the end, Schmisek also offers some philosophical points of reference for thinking about it all, putting special emphasis on the human penchant for creating meaning.

This book obviously will be of keen interest in academic circles, and I can see it on the required reading lists of religious studies, philosophy, and theology departments for years to come. Yet I would suggest that it also deserves a much wider audience, among journalists, policy analysts, political leaders, diplomats, geopolitical experts, and military and security officials—really, anyone who's seriously interested in understanding how an extremely large swath of the human population is likely to interpret, and therefore react, to the events that are allegedly their specialty. Of course, we can all decide for ourselves how to interpret reality, but we don't get to make that decision for anyone else. If we want to understand what's happening in the world, we simply cannot ignore the categories within which so many people think.

I've known Brian Schmisek for a fairly long stretch of time, and I've always found him to be level headed, fair minded, and wise in addition to intelligent. (Of course, intelligence is no measure of virtue, but wisdom certainly is.) Those qualities are all amply on display in these pages. I've never had the pleasure of taking a class from Brian, but I've always imagined he must be an outstanding teacher, and this book is confirmation of the point. Here, however, his classroom isn't confined to a physical space and maybe thirty restless undergrads itching to get back to the lake—he does, after all, teach in Minnesota, the "land of 10,000 lakes"—but rather, his classroom is formed by anyone with eyes to see and ears to hear.

Actually, if I were so inclined, I might even see *Signs, Superstitions, and God's Plan* as an act of Divine Providence, God's chosen instrument for giving us just the right interpretive key at just the right historical moment. While that's the kind of spiritualized hermeneutic of which I'm normally a bit dubious, after you read this engaging and deeply thoughtful book, you just might find yourself wondering the same thing.

PREFACE

On September 11, 2001, New York City skies were bright blue, and the air was crisp and cool. The terrorist attacks early that morning clashed starkly with the promise of a new, cloudless day. Dread and panic spread across the nation with news of thousands dead.

Not long after that terrible tragedy, some preachers and religious thought leaders began attributing that awful event to the violation of God's principles by the United States. As a result, their thinking went, God had allowed the country to suffer the attack.

> I really believe that the pagans, and the abortionists, and the feminists, and the gays and the lesbians who are actively trying to make that an alternative lifestyle, the ACLU, People for the American Way, all of them who have tried to secularize America. I point the finger in their face and say "you helped this happen."
>
> Falwell, pastor of the 22,000-member Thomas Road Baptist Church, viewed the attacks as God's judgment on America for "throwing God out of the public square, out of the schools. The abortionists have got to bear some burden for this because God will not be mocked."[1]

Falwell later apologized saying, "I would never blame any human being except the terrorists, and if I left that impression with gays or lesbians or anyone else, I apologize."[2] Still the sentiment that God punished the United States as a country on 9/11 was echoed by others[3] and continued most recently by Republican Roy Moore, a candidate for one of Alabama's seats in the U.S. Senate. He suggested on February 5, 2017, that "God was upset at the United States because 'we legitimize sodomy' and 'legitimize abortion.'"[4]

Tragedy frequently brings out desperate needs to discern meaning. Too often tragedy is ascribed to God, or even to God's punishment for human behavior, as we see above. Some attributed God's activity not only to 9/11 but to Hurricane Katrina as well. And such divine attribution happens nearly every time we witness a tragedy. We do not need to look far to find someone attributing the cause of a calamity to God's anger, God's plan, or even God's wisdom. Sometimes, God is even said to have allowed the tragedy because of bad or sinful human behavior.

On April 4, 2020, not long after the COVID-19 shutdown of the U.S. economy, Christian evangelist Franklin Graham was asked about the pandemic by Fox News host Jeanine Pirro, "How could God allow this thing to happen?" Graham responded, "Well, I don't think it's God's plan for this to happen. It's because of the sin that's in the world. Man has turned his back on God, we have sinned against him, and we need to ask for God's forgiveness and that's what Easter's all about."[5]

Many such statements and theological explanations are widely and rightly dismissed in a secular culture, but is there a plan or some greater reason why things happen the way they do? And if so, how far developed is that plan? Does it involve big-picture issues only, or does it extend to everyone personally? And if there is a divine plan for each person, how detailed is it? Is there a person destined to be my "soul mate" that I will find if I follow a divine plan? Can I disrupt or otherwise frustrate God's plan by not cooperating? Are any children I might or might not have part of God's plan, too? Does God's plan extend to what route I might take to work each day, or what I might have for breakfast? Or is the divine plan not bothered with such details? If "God's plan" sounds too religious, what about providence, destiny, or fate? How detailed might that be? And if even that sounds too spiritual, doesn't "everything happen for a reason"? When something serendipitous happens, it's easy to believe it was "meant to be."

There is a cottage industry for books explaining reasons or giving meaning to events in daily life. If we narrow the focus from a nation to a family, or even a person, we recognize that these questions of meaning usually arise in moments of crisis or opportunity. We struggle to ascertain meaning in the face of the loss of a child, a tragic accident, or natural disasters. New opportunities can be ascribed to fate, God's plan, or simply being in the right place at the right time. The ancients had the same struggle in determining the actions of the universe on human affairs, and they asked many of the same questions we do.

Homer's *Odyssey*, the classic epic about the interactions of gods, goddesses, women, and men, tells the harrowing journey of Odysseus from the Trojan War back to his home. The trek was fraught with danger, which accompanied him from the beginning. But the trek was also enhanced by the protection of certain gods and goddesses. Even the time of his return, though chosen by the gods themselves, was permeated with danger. That is, despite the gods favoring Odysseus, and choosing a start time as it were, Odysseus himself was not free from danger. And so begins a primeval tale about divine action in the lives of humanity.

> Tell me, O Muse, of the man of many devices, who wandered full many ways after he had sacked the sacred citadel of Troy. Many were the men whose

cities he saw and whose mind he learned, aye, and many the woes he suffered in his heart upon the sea, seeking to win his own life and the return of his comrades. Yet even so he saved not his comrades, though he desired it sore, for through their own blind folly they perished—fools, who devoured the kine of Helios Hyperion; but he took from them the day of their returning. Of these things, goddess, daughter of Zeus, beginning where thou wilt, tell thou even unto us.

Now all the rest, as many as had escaped sheer destruction, were at home, safe from both war and sea, but Odysseus alone, filled with longing for his return and for his wife, did the queenly nymph Calypso, that bright goddess, keep back in her hollow caves, yearning that he should be her husband. But when, as the seasons revolved, the year came in which *the gods had ordained that he should return home* to Ithaca, not even there was he free from toils, even among his own folk. And all the gods pitied him save Poseidon; but he continued to rage unceasingly against godlike Odysseus until at length he reached his own land.[6] [italics mine]

Though the ancient world is replete with references to the divine, fate, the will of the gods, and other actions that seemed beyond the realm of human control, this phenomenon is not restricted to the ancient world. For example, at the 2016 Republican National Convention, Eric Trump was about to make a momentous speech only to have the teleprompter go down. For fifteen minutes, he was afraid he would have to "wing it," when the teleprompter suddenly turned on again. He attributed this "miracle" to the prayer of Paula White, an evangelical pastor from Orlando. Asked later about this turn of events that evening, White said, "I probably [interceded] against any plot or plan or weapon of the enemy to interfere with the plan or the will of God."[7]

In the case of Sarah Palin, she attributed to God the fact that she was disinvited from giving a speech introducing Newt Gingrich to the National Republican Senatorial Committee on June 8, 2010. The day before, upon learning that she was no longer speaking, she wrote in an email, "Yes, [Newt/GOP] are egotistical, narrow minded machine goons...but all the more reason God protected me from getting up on stage in front of 5000 political and media 'elites' to praise him, then it be shown across the nation."[8] "Plus, I had nothing to wear, and God knew that too."[9]

Discerning the plans of the gods or simply attributing events to God's plan or intervention has been part of the human condition for centuries up to and including today, and not only from conservative thinkers and politicians. In 2018, Canadian rapper Drake even released a number one song entitled "God's Plan," about his own fame and fate. Billy Preston had a 1969 hit, "That's the Way God Planned It." We have many names, categories, and ways of speaking about this phenomenon of serendipity, and not all invoke the divine. Some do attribute serendipitous events to the divine and speak of God's will, plan, purpose, or more generally, providence. Others look to the universe and speak of fate or destiny, which may or may not be preceded by oracles, signs, or omens. Still others have more generic explanations, reflected in sayings such as, "Everything happens for a reason," or "It was meant to be."

We will explore these categories over the course of eight short chapters, showing how the ancient world (including the biblical world) expressed these ideas that have been used throughout history and still resonate today. The chapters are arranged topically, and each uses a variety of examples. The first chapter discusses God's plan, will, or purpose, with special attention paid to the ubiquitous term *God's plan*. The second chapter addresses providence with examples from the classical world and American history. Chapter 3 discusses destiny and fate, illustrated primarily by the ancient world's use of oracles. Chapter 4 broadens the discussion to include signs and omens; whereas chapter 5 speaks of natural wonders and some ways they have been interpreted. Chapter 6 is a brief chapter on superstition, followed by a chapter on the less theologically based maxim, "Everything happens for a reason." The last chapter engages various thought experiments that ultimately invite the reader to consider the very human activity of meaning making. Some closing thoughts wrap up the discussion in a conclusion followed by a brief epilogue. This short work shows that we in the modern world use many of the same categories we inherited from antiquity to make sense of the world and to interpret events in meaningful ways. Yet, now with a more modern understanding of how the world functions, the reader is invited to consider a radically different way of thinking, one that recognizes the central and fundamental role that the individual plays in making meaning for oneself.

For the purpose of this book, we will not make judgments about whether something happened according to God's will, plan, or purpose, though many people do in fact make these judgments. We will instead see how people find meaning from those attributions. In other words, one does not have to believe in God to see and recognize that other people believe in God. When a remarkable or opportune thing happens, the one who does not believe in God will not attribute it to God, whereas the believer will likely do just that. In this book, we will respect the point of view of believers but will not make affirmative or negative judgments about those claims. The reader is left to do that for him or herself. Still, we will examine some of the claims made by believers and nonbelievers alike and see how they stand up under closer scrutiny.

In the ancient world, many things were thought to be actions of the gods. The classic "god of the gaps" comes to mind, wherein God or the gods are used to explain the unexplainable, to explain the "gap" in knowledge. For example, early humans did not know what caused thunder and many surmised that it must be caused by a god. Norse mythology called that god Thor, whereas the early Germans called that god Donar.[10] And so, we get the name of the day of the week, Thursday, from "Thor's Day." Once human beings had a better understanding of thunder and lightning, the god of that knowledge gap receded, and we no longer ascribe thunder to Thor or Donar. The kind of theology that postulates a god to explain the "gaps" in our own knowledge inevitably reduces god to a smaller and smaller entity, who performs fewer and fewer actions whose causes are unknown. With the frontiers of knowledge being stretched and pushed daily, any "god of the gaps" is pushed further and further away as well. So, in the end, the god of the gaps becomes infinitesimal, if there is a need for such a god at all.

But our discussion is not focused on a god of the gaps. Instead, we want to examine what is referred to as God's will, plan, or purpose. In antiquity, gods were not only used to explain the unknown, but they were seen to guide events according to a purpose. We saw above that Homer spoke of the gods' choosing the time of Odysseus's journey; such a concept was used widely in the ancient world. For many, the gods were intimately involved in the lives of humans. The constellation of closely related terms to speak of this includes not only *will*, *purpose*, and *plan*, but also *divination* (or its Greek counterpart, *mantikē*) and *providence* (or its Greek counterpart, *pronoia*). *Providence* ("foresight" or "seeing ahead") meant the ability (usually of the divine) to know the future or at least events in the future. When a human being was made aware of this divine foresight, he or she was sometimes said to possess the gift of prophecy.

Rome's most famous orator, Cicero (106–43 BCE), wrote a treatise on divination (*De Divinatione*) in two books. He defined *divination* as "the foreknowledge and foretelling of events that happen by chance." Roughly speaking, the first book, in the voice of Cicero's brother, Quintus, consists of arguments in favor of divination. We will refer to this as the protagonist position. Cicero (in the voice of Quintus) classifies divination into two broad categories: artificial (astrology, portents, lightning and thunder, etc.) and natural (dreams, prophecies such as the Delphic and other oracles, etc.). In the second book, Cicero himself argues against divination, claiming that there is no use for it. We will refer to this as the position of the antagonist. Cicero says that it is "not in the power even of God himself to know what event is going to happen accidentally and by chance. For if he knows, then the event is certain to happen; but if it is certain to happen, chance does not exist. And yet, chance does exist, therefore there is no foreknowledge of things that happen by chance."[11] This classical text tells us much about the way some ancient Romans thought about the world. Examples from this work will inform our own study below. But it will be important to recognize whether the piece quoted from *De Divinatione* is from the position of the protagonist (Quintus) in book 1, or that of the antagonist (Cicero himself) in book 2.

About a hundred years after the time of Cicero, in the first century of the common era and only a few decades after the crucifixion of Jesus, many Jews revolted against the Romans. In the initial stages of the rebellion they made tremendous strides, destroying an entire Roman legion of about six thousand soldiers. It was then that the emperor Nero sent one of his best generals, Vespasian, to put down the uprising. Vespasian was accompanied by his two militaristic sons, Titus and Domitian, with Titus second in command.

Josephus (ca. 37–ca. 100 CE) led the Jewish forces in Galilee, the same district where Jesus had come from, and was eventually pinned down in the town of Jotapata, where he was under siege for about six weeks during the summer of 67 CE. When it was clear that the Jewish defenders were going to be overrun by the Romans led by Vespasian, they made a deadly pact. The Jewish soldiers preferred to die at the hands of one another than to die at the hands of a Roman. They agreed to draw lots, with one person killing another until only one remained who would commit suicide. And so it happened that Josephus and another were the last two. At that point, Josephus convinced his fellow that they should both turn themselves over to the Romans that they might both live. And in that manner Josephus escaped death and attributed it to "chance or the providence of God."[12] We might also say the episode could have been attributed to the conniving manner of Josephus himself!

Josephus's escape allowed him the chance to eventually ingratiate himself with the Romans, particularly with Vespasian. How he did that is a fascinating story. After being captured and led to Vespasian, Josephus told him that there were prophecies that foretold that the Messiah, the ruler of the world, would come from Galilee. Josephus said that this applied to Vespasian, who was intrigued by the idea. (Christians of course believed that the prophecies applied to Jesus). So, Vespasian kept Josephus available (in prison) and used him as an interpreter when he eventually laid siege to Jerusalem.

The Emperor Nero committed suicide in 69 CE, which launched a civil war with various generals vying for power. That year was known as "the year of four emperors" with Vespasian himself being the fourth. When Vespasian became emperor in 69 CE, it seemed that the prophecies of Josephus had in fact been accurate. Vespasian was the prophesied Messiah; the ruler of the world had in fact come from Galilee. Vespasian then left his son Titus to finish the siege of Jerusalem, ending in its destruction.

Vespasian reigned as Emperor until 79 CE, when he died and was succeeded by his son Titus, who reigned for only two years and was succeeded by Domitian. Together they were known as the Flavian dynasty and were renowned for such monuments as the Flavian Amphitheater (also known as the Colosseum) and the Arch of Titus, which was erected to commemorate the Roman victory over the Jewish people. Both the Colosseum and the Arch of Titus still stand today as testaments to this powerful family and the Roman people. As the Romans saw it, their god, Jupiter Optimus Maximus (the best, the greatest), had defeated the god of the Jewish people. Even the reliefs in the Arch of Titus depict the Romans parading a menorah and other symbols of Jewish identity in a triumph (the parade of a victorious general through the streets of Rome). Likewise, obelisks in Rome were taken from Egyptian cities demonstrating Roman power.

Back to Josephus, who found that he was favored; he took the name Titus Flavius, and he lived a life of relative leisure, writing an account of the war aptly titled *Jewish Wars*, and other works including *The Antiquities of the Jews*. So, was Josephus spared by God's providence? Was he spared by his own craftiness? Or was there some blend of the two? Was Vespasian the long-awaited Messiah from Galilee who would rule over the world? Was Jupiter Optimus Maximus really more powerful than the god of the Jewish people? In the 70s of the first century, it certainly seemed so to the Romans.

ACKNOWLEDGMENTS

Throughout college and graduate school, I entertained common and perpetual questions about the meaning of life. Was there a plan to follow? Was I meant to meet someone? Have a family? What was my destiny? How might I have an insight into providence and conform my life accordingly? Might I confound or frustrate any larger design by making a "wrong" choice? In many respects, this book is something I would like to have read at that point in my life. It's a book for my twenty-year-old self. The questions that perplexed me then still provide rich food for thought today; they will exhaust me before I exhaust them.

Over the course of the last five or so years, I have noted various stories in articles, books, movies, and the like that might reference God's plan, providence, fate, superstition, and more. Many reflected themes like those in the ancient world and throughout history. And there were certainly many more stories than I could use here, just as the reader has many more. There were many kind interlocutors, and I shared early drafts of the manuscript with friends and family who offered feedback. Some of these people include Michael DeBartolo, Brother Robert Smith, FSC, PhD, Michelle Arnold, and Jim McGill. Catherine Putonti, PhD, at Loyola University Chicago read a short section on biology and offered insightful comment. Librarians at Saint Mary's University of Minnesota and one Rachel McPherson from the Longview Public Library in Texas were generous and helpful in finding materials for me. And Donna Crilly at Paulist Press was a responsive and accessible editor, upbeat and energetic for the project. Her assistance made the work come together quickly.

An indispensable life partner and muse is Marnie, who continually makes me see things anew, often posing fundamental questions that strike to the heart of the matter. After having spent more than half of our lives together, her companionship, kindness, generosity, and enduring love have been central to who I have become. The life we created together is beyond what could have been imagined in those years when questions about providence and God's plan preoccupied my thoughts. This book is for her and in many ways because of her.

Chapter One

GOD'S PLAN, WILL, OR PURPOSE

The concept of God's plan permeates today's culture. We don't need to look far to find the term in popular use. Anyone who consumes modern media has likely seen a tag line for the website christianmingle.com, which is, "God has a plan for each one of us,"[1] or "find God's match for you." It's been noted that the quick growth of the website was fueled in large part by its God campaign.[2] The audience for such a site is certainly self-selecting. One presumes that those looking for God's role in a "match" are more likely to visit the site and use it than those who are not. But not every match is made in heaven. At least one pastor has entertained the idea that God may want you to leave your marriage.[3] So the idea of God's plan is not restricted to relationships. Some believe that even the oil and natural gas in the earth that are extracted and refined for human use are there as part of God's plan.[4]

WAR

There are no atheists in foxholes.

—Unknown

SIGNS, SUPERSTITIONS, AND GOD'S PLAN

Often, in the chaos and tumult of war, soldiers and their leaders may ascribe actions and events to God's plan. In only one such example, the military historian Beevor says that on Christmas Eve during the Battle of the Bulge a chaplain said, "Do not plan, for God's plan will prevail."[5] One woman wrote, "We feel like we are in God's hand and we surrender ourselves to it." Beevor adds, "The Walloons were largely Catholic and deeply religious. Committing themselves to the hands of the Almighty was undoubtedly a comfort, when they had so little control over their own fate. Reciting the rosary together helped dull the pain of individual fear, and calm the nerves."[6]

Interpreting events as part of "God's plan" makes a strong theological claim. The language about God's plan is heard in occasions of war, ancient, modern, and throughout history. But how detailed is God's plan? In terms of war, is it for one side to win? Or does God's plan extend to each individual soldier and bystander, each bullet and fragment? A troubling and sad episode for one family of civilians at Christmas during the same Battle of the Bulge illustrates the problem:

> But the festival [Christmas] brought little joy to the Belgian population of the Ardennes. In a village close to Elsenborn, where fighting had died down, the Gronsfeld family decided to come out of their cellar to celebrate Christmas Day. The light was blinding with the sun reflecting off the snow as they sat at the kitchen table, father, mother, and their young daughter, Elfriede. Suddenly, a German shell exploded near by, sending a sliver of shrapnel through the window. It cut deep into Elfriede Gronsfeld's neck. American medics came to her aid, but there was nothing they could do. The girl was buried on December 29. She was five years old. "What can one say to the mother?" One of the village's women

mourned in her diary. "She cries and cannot understand."[7]

Tragedy abounds in this world of ours, and especially so during war. Bystanders are victims of random acts of violence. Children are not spared this violence as the story above illustrates. Indeed, there are countless examples of tragic violence throughout history and unfortunately many more recent examples. No doubt the reader can think of many examples quickly and easily and, if not from war, then from regular accidental events in daily life. Is each according to God's plan?

During the U.S. Civil War, President Abraham Lincoln, himself a believer, pondered the role of God's will, as the following from September 1862 shows.

The will of God prevails. In great contests each party claims to act in accordance with the will of God. Both may be, and one must be wrong. God can not be for, and against the same thing at the same time. In the present civil war it is quite possible that God's purpose is something different from the purpose of either party—and yet the human instrumentalities, working just as they do, are of the best adaptation to effect His purpose. I am almost ready to say this is probably true—that God wills this contest, and wills that it shall not end yet. By his mere quiet power, on the minds of the now contestants, He could have either saved or destroyed the Union without a human contest. Yet the contest began. And having begun He could give the final victory to either side any day. Yet the contest proceeds.[8]

Another quote along these same lines is often attributed to Lincoln and displays his deep sense of humility: "My concern is

3

not whether God is on our side; my greatest concern is to be on God's side, for God is always right." Though these words are not in the collected works of Lincoln, they come from Francis B. Carpenter's 1867 work, *Six Months in the White House with Abraham Lincoln*. His telling of the story is that a clergyman expressed his hope that "the Lord was on our side." "I am not at all concerned about that," replied Mr. Lincoln, "for I know that the Lord is *always* on the side of the *right*. But it is my constant anxiety and prayer that *I* and *this nation* should be on the Lord's *side*" (italics in the original).[9] The desire of Lincoln to be on God's side rather than wondering whether God is on his side is one of the many qualities that marked him as a unique leader, one to be admired and emulated. Sarah Palin on the other hand was adamant in June 2008 that the United States' war in Iraq was a task from God: "Our national leaders are sending them out on a task that is from God. That's what we have to make sure that we're praying for, that there is a plan and that plan is God's plan."[10] Interestingly, in the same address, Palin claimed that a proposed $30 billion natural gas pipeline in Alaska was "God's will."

More recently, after the U.S. military pullout from Syria in 2019, Omar, a Palestinian refugee who grew up in Syria, said, "Maybe the Americans rule the world today, but God Almighty promised the Muslims that, in the end, the world will be ruled by Islam."[11] There can be a great comfort in believing or "knowing" that God promises victory to your group, nation, religion, people, tribe, or point of view.

LEADERS

Providence has given us this victory.

—President William Henry Harrison

> Providence hadn't a damn thing to do with it. A number of men were compelled to approach the penitentiary to make him President.
>
> —Harrison's campaign manager

William Henry Harrison served the shortest Presidential term in history after dying on his thirty-first day in office on April 4, 1841.

Going back to antiquity, to the time of the Egyptian pharaohs, there has been a notion of divine right of kingship, that the king was on the throne because of God's will. In the ancient world, kings, pharaohs, and various leaders were thought to be divine, or at least sons of God (Pss 2:7; 89:27–28; 110:2–3; 2 Sam 7:14). Some people today easily dismiss such notions as representative of a bygone age. But it might be humbling to recognize that it was not until the renaissance and the spirit of revolution in the Americas and then in France that the idea of the "divine right of kings" was thrown off by force. The American experiment of self-government was itself decried by the Roman Catholic Church, and eventually condemned as "Americanism."[12] That condemnation by the Church and its way of looking at secular societies was not changed officially until Vatican II and its 1965 document on "religious liberty," commonly known as the decree on religious freedom (*Dignitatis Humanae*). Even today, there seems to be something in the human spirit that wants to believe or know that leaders are in their role because of providence.

In the United States, many Trump supporters say that God wanted him to be president.[13] Not merely President Trump's supporters, but the leaders of his movement see divine action at work. For example, Franklin Graham says, "Trump is president for a reason. God put Trump there."[14] Scott Pruitt, the former Secretary of the Interior who resigned under a cloud of scandal, said that Trump was president because of God's providence.[15] Vice President Pence also sees God's plan at work in the election of the Trump-Pence ticket. "If you're Mike Pence, and you believe what he believes, you know God had a plan," says Ralph Reed, an evangelical power broker and a friend of the vice president.[16]

Sarah Palin, the Republican vice presidential candidate in 2008, put her election "in God's hands, that the right thing for America will be done at the end of the day on November 4."[17] Rick Perry, former Energy Secretary in the Trump administration and two-term Texas governor, says Trump (and Obama) were "ordained by God" to be president.[18] Others couch their language with a bit more caution, or perhaps to explain a geopolitical reason for God's action. For example, then-Secretary of State Mike Pompeo said that it was possible that God raised up President Trump to protect Israel from Iranian aggression.[19] One wonders if Trump supporters believe Divine Providence was at work in every U.S. election for president or only that which produced President Trump. We might also wonder whether Sarah Palin believed that "the right thing for America" was done on November 4, 2008, and what that might say in her mind about God.

Those who see divine action in political campaigns do not limit themselves to U.S. presidents. Sarah Palin contemplated a run for Alaska senator in the 2022 race, saying, "If God wants me to do it, I will."[20] The former California Governor Arnold Schwarzenegger saw his successful run to be governor as part of God's plan.[21] And when politicians lose, that can be understood as God's plan too. The Wisconsin state supreme court incumbent Daniel Kelly conceded the race saying, "It has been the highest honor of my career to serve the people of Wisconsin on their Supreme Court these past four years. Obviously I had hoped my service would continue for another decade, but tonight's results make clear that God has a different plan for my future."[22]

As we saw above, the sixteenth president of the United States was humble and more circumspect in claiming certainty in knowing God's plan, or even knowing what is right, as his second inaugural demonstrates:

> With malice toward none; with charity for all; with firmness in the right, as God gives us to see the right, let us strive on to finish the work we are in; to bind up the nation's wounds; to care for him who shall have borne the battle, and for his widow, and his orphan—to do all which may achieve and cherish a just, and a lasting peace, among ourselves, and with all nations.[23]

Here, in one of the most famous presidential inaugural speeches, delivered in 1864 after years of civil war and tens of thousands dead and many more wounded, Lincoln seems almost to hedge, "with firmness in the right," for it is only, "as God gives us to see the right." How different the speech would be if it did not include the clause "as God gives us to see the right." It wouldn't be Lincoln. But it is precisely because of his humility while bearing the mantle of leadership amid crisis that his words, "as God gives us to see the right," become so powerful.

Aside from leaders in times of crisis, war, or no crises at all, there are many others who will claim to know God's will or plan for individuals that reaches down into their very state of life.

STATES OF LIFE

The term *God's plan* can be used by religious people, and often it seems to be used in a way to maintain the status quo.

Though the scriptures are filled with instances that could be used to undermine the argument for each, often "God's plan" is used by modern Christians to refer to states of life such as marriage, the roles of women and men, the impermissibility of same-sex relationships, or even in a way to promote celibacy. For example, Genesis 1:26 speaks of God creating humanity male and female. Many evangelicals and Catholics[24] will claim that because of this verse and the initial couple (there are no other humans mentioned), marriage was ordained by God to be a relationship between a man and a woman. Some evangelicals will shorten this to say, "God made Adam and Eve, not Adam and Steve." Of course, much of the Old Testament, to say nothing of the New Testament, portrays countless examples of polygamy, divorce, incest, premarital and extramarital affairs, prostitution, and much more. "God's plan for marriage" seems to have been an ideal in Genesis 1, and ever since. In addition to marriage, some claim there is also "God's plan for biblical womanhood."[25] Often it seems that by claiming some state of life is "God's plan," those making the claim are likely defending a status quo, or even a status quo that seems to be slipping away.

Sometimes the term *plan of God* goes beyond marriage, beyond women, and is applied to gays and lesbians, even by educated theologians. One recent example illustrates the point. According to the July 16, 2017, edition of the *New York Times*, "Two very different books about being Roman Catholic and gay were released recently, each with an endorsement from a cardinal who oversees an archdiocese along the Hudson River." Cardinal Joseph W. Tobin, the archbishop of Newark, endorsed *Building a Bridge*, calling it "brave, prophetic and inspiring." The book calls on church leaders to use preferred terms like *gay* instead of *same-sex attraction*, as a sign of respect to gay Catholics.

Cardinal Timothy M. Dolan, the archbishop of New York, endorsed "Why I Don't Call Myself Gay," a memoir by a Catholic man who resisted his homosexual attractions and who now leads a celibate life inspired by the gospel. Cardinal Dolan praised the book as an "honest account of the genuine struggles faced by those with same-sex attraction" that details how its author came to "understand and accept God's loving plan for his life."[26]

It is not so unique that cardinals (there are only about two hundred or so in the world)[27] would take different approaches to a divisive issue. But it seems astonishing that one cardinal would speak of a celibate gay man as accepting "God's loving plan for his life,"[28] and thereby seeming so comfortable in claiming to know what God's plan is for a whole group of people.

But nowhere is it more apparent that the claim of "God's plan" might serve merely to defend a status quo, than when we move beyond our own immediate context and consider the American institution of slavery. Unfortunately, many defenders of slavery referred to it as God's plan, foreordained by the divine.[29] Nothing in Scripture seems to condemn slavery. The Constitution accepted it, as the Three-Fifths Compromise indicates. So, with divine and constitutional support of such an institution as slavery, how then could any American move against it? Here, too, it seems the claim of God's plan or God's will was invoked to protect the status quo.

For some who believe in a celestial realm where forces of good and evil fight it out on earth, much like armies on a field of battle, God's plan is opposed by Satan's plan. These kinds of ideas are repeated today, as illustrated by a recent case. In 2017, the nomination of Jeff Mateer for a U.S. federal judgeship was derailed when it was revealed that two years earlier he had said that transgender children were part of "Satan's plan."[30] For some, the idea that there is a master plan to which one conforms or another against which one fights might provide meaning and purpose. In the case of Jeff Mateer, he continued in that same speech to say that same-sex marriage was "disgusting." Such a worldview can be reinforced by attributing "disgusting" things to that which is part of Satan's plan. They mutually reinforce each other: what is disgusting is part of Satan's plan and Satan's plan is to promote what is disgusting. But attributing actions to Satan's plan tells us more about those who would make that attribution, rather than telling us much about a celestial force opposed to the divine.

CLASSICAL WORLD

The attribution of various human activities and natural events to divine forces has deep roots in human history. In the Aegean Sea, the Greek island of Samothrace was a place of devotion in antiquity, the place of a temple to the "great gods." According to the third-century-CE biographer Diogenes Laertius, after a certain shipwreck, those sailors who survived wrote notes of thanks in the temple at Samothrace, praising the gods who saved them. One snarky fellow (also by the name of Diogenes [404–323 BCE], a contemporary of Plato) commented in reply, "There would have been more if those who were not saved had written some offerings."[31]

This comment reflects something central to the notion of being "saved" by the gods or some other supernatural or divine power. What about those who were not "saved"? Only those who survived the shipwreck can claim to be saved. The logic is circular and lends itself to still further questions. Why were some saved and not others? Did the gods show favor to some and not others? If so, why? Surely those who perished would have written notes of thanks if they too had survived. From the pithy remark by our ancient snark quoted above, we see that such theological or philosophical riddles piqued the curiosity of minds from centuries ago as well as our own.

For some ancient philosophers there was no riddle whatsoever. The naturalist, philosopher, and writer Pliny the Elder

(23–79 CE), who lived an illustrious life, had no patience for those who thought that a supreme being (God) would oversee human affairs. In fact, Pliny stated it quite plainly when he said, "That a supreme being pays attention to human affairs is a ridiculous notion. Can we believe that it would not be defiled by such a disagreeable and so multifarious a duty?"[32]

For Pliny, it is as though the supreme being would not be bothered with such things as human affairs. Even so, the idea that there is a benevolent force gently guiding events can be a form of solace for many if not most. And for much of the Classical world, there was a deep sense of Divine Providence, fate, and foreknowledge. This sense was shared by the authors of the Old Testament as well.

BIBLE

Most if not all authors of the scriptures saw events about which they were writing to be disclosures of God's providence, God's will, or God's plan. From the opening verses of Genesis where God says, "Let there be light," we see a disclosure of God's will. God wishes there to be light and light springs into being. So, the entire Bible can be said to be a revelation of God's will. Broadly speaking, God's will in much of the Old Testament is essentially that God's people follow Torah. By so doing, the people will prosper. Even so, there are Old Testament passages cited often today to speak of God's will. Two of the more famous passages in the Old Testament that speak of God's plan, as they form the basis of much popular theology today, are Jeremiah 29:11 and Isaiah 46:10.

Most of the Old Testament was written in Hebrew, and when it was translated into Greek prior to the time of Jesus, two of the more prominent but certainly not the only terms used to translate these interrelated concepts were *boulē* (plan) and *thelēma* (will). Another Greek term used, but not as prominently as *boulē* and *thelēma*, is *logismon*, which can mean "plan," but also "thought" or "argument/speculation." In the New Testament, which was composed entirely in Greek by various authors, the term *thelēma* was used most often to speak of God's design. But significantly, Luke is the New Testament author who used and promoted the term *boulē*.

Jeremiah 29:11

Jeremiah 29:1–23 preserves a letter to the Babylonian exiles from Jeremiah himself. Different groups of exiles were taken into captivity after the fall of Jerusalem in 597 BCE and its destruction ten years later, each event at the hands of Nebuchadnezzar II, king of the Babylonian Empire. Jeremiah wrote to the exiles to inspire hope; in the same letter he spoke an "oracle of the LORD" (vv. 10–14 NABRE) promising blessing and welfare for the exiles, which would be fulfilled after seventy years. This promise of a future restoration is part of "God's plan." "For surely I know the plans I have for you, says the LORD, plans for your welfare and not for harm, to give you a future with hope" (v. 11). Here the Greek word that is translating the Hebrew term for *plan* is *logismon*.[33] It is used both as a verb (I plan to...) and as a noun (plans [for your welfare]). This was meant to comfort the exiles with the knowledge that God had a plan to bring them back to the land, to a future of hope, not a woeful exilic existence. And when Cyrus, the king of Persia, defeated Babylon in 539 BCE, the exiles were permitted to return to their native land. This prophecy from Jeremiah expresses an idea similar to the one in the ancient world that God (the gods) does indeed have plans, designs, counsel, and foreknowledge. This passage has become a favorite of those preaching the "prosperity gospel" today, which essentially says good things happen to those who are good.[34] Often when the passage is cited today it is stripped of its historical context. Instead, it's read to mean that God has a plan for every person to have a future of hope, which is a beautiful and inspiring idea. But it's not what the passage meant when Jeremiah wrote it.

Isaiah 46:9–10

Scholars maintain that chapters 40—55 of Isaiah were written around the same time as Jeremiah 29. The message consoles the people in their Babylonian exile. However, it is no longer Isaiah who writes (he composed chaps. 1—39 from between 742–701 BCE), but an anonymous poet (also known as Deutero-Isaiah or Second Isaiah) who says prophetically,

> For I am God, and there is no other;
>   I am God, and there is no one like me,
> declaring the end from the beginning
>   and from ancient times things not yet done,
> saying, "My purpose [*boulē*]³⁵ shall stand,
>   and I will fulfill my intention [*bebouleumai*]."

This claim that God foretells the outcome of events and that God's purpose or plan stands is akin to a classical view in antiquity. In this case from Deutero-Isaiah, divine foreknowledge is not attributed to an amorphous deity but to God, for there is no other, none like God. The Greek term for *plan* here is that used by the Gospel of Luke, *boulē*. The passage from Isaiah, like that from Jeremiah above, is applied regularly by modern preachers to individuals, which is beyond the scope of the text when it was first written. Even so, this broader application of ancient, scriptural texts happens quite often. Preachers have a gift for taking verses out of context to make them say something else, supporting the point he or she wants to make. Because the Bible can be cherry-picked and made to say anything, a friend of mine is fond of saying, "Give me the Bible and thirty minutes and I'll make up any religion you want."

Today, most scripture scholars recognize that discerning the meaning of the author, also known as the historical-critical method, is an essential task of exegesis. The Catholic Church itself makes this claim: "The historical-critical method is the indispensable method for the scientific study of the meaning of ancient texts."[36] The Jesuit theologian so instrumental at Vatican II, Karl Rahner (1904–84), seemed to recognize this shift when he is reported to have said that based on the work of scripture scholars, theologians were no longer able to read and apply scripture as they did, "in den guten alten Zeiten" (in the good old days).

The Old Testament background to the term *God's will* or *God's plan* thus set the stage for some New Testament authors who interpreted the life and events of Jesus as fulfilling God's will. To speak of the "divine will" or "divine plan," these New Testament authors would have recourse to one of these two terms—*boulē* (plan, purpose) and *thelēma* (will, wish, desire). The clear favorite for most of the New Testament authors was *thelēma*.

Luke-Acts

When we shift our attention to the New Testament, which was written entirely in Greek, though *thelēma* was used more frequently overall, Luke used *boulē*, "God's plan" or a variant thereof, more than any other New Testament author. He seems to have found in it a worthy concept to convey his understanding of what God had done in Christ. That is, the events that unfolded only a generation before Luke would be expressed by him as having happened according to "God's plan." This articulation gives meaning to the tragic events of Jesus's passion and death. Luke presents the events in a way that can be more readily understood. What Paul called "foolishness to the Gentiles" (1 Cor 1:23), the crucified Christ, is presented by Luke as part of a larger, divine "plan" that encompasses even more than the betrayal, suffering, death, and resurrection of Jesus, and the Pentecost event. For Luke, God's plan extended back at least a millennium, to the time of David (Acts 2) and it continues past the time of Jesus to Paul's conversion (Acts 22:14; 26:16).[37]

The term *plan of God* seems to have been used by Luke to appeal to his Hellenized audience. Luke expressed the Christian message with fidelity to the scriptures and to what God had done in Jesus and translated that message into terms his audience would recognize and accept. By using the term *plan of God*, Luke effectively recovered and utilized an Old Testament term that would also mean something to them. Unlike a mere stenographer, Luke is a theologian in his own right. He found a convenient term to express the meaning of the events that unfolded a generation before him. For Luke, God's plan encompasses David, the ministry of John the Baptist, Jesus himself as well as his betrayal, death, and resurrection in Jerusalem, the outpouring of the Spirit at Pentecost, and the preaching and ministry of the early Christians, including Paul. These events fulfill a determined plan according to the foreknowledge of God. No other New Testament author makes such a sustained case.

GOD'S PLAN OF SALVATION

The simplicity of the term *God's plan* became programmatic for later Church fathers, catechisms, and preaching down to our present day. Once Luke established the overarching concept of "God's plan," to give meaning to the life, death, and resurrection of Jesus, Church fathers took it up and expanded its use widely,[38] especially in catechetics, the teaching of the faith. In some ways, this reaches a pinnacle in the second edition of the *Catechism of the Catholic Church* (*CCC*).[39]

In that 1997 work, we see that sections 751–80, entitled "The Church in God's Plan" is explicit that the church is part of the plan of the Holy Trinity (§758), a plan born in the Father's heart (§759), a "plan of salvation" (§763, see also §§841, 851). The Church is said to be the "visible plan of God's love for humanity" (§776) and both the "means and goal of God's plan" (§778).

After the promulgation of the *CCC*, local and national conferences of bishops were encouraged to develop their own catechisms (as stated in the *CCC* itself). So, shortly after the *CCC*, the *United States Catholic Catechism for Adults* (*USCCA*) was developed and published.[40] A simple search for the term *plan* in the *USCCA* shows that the term permeates the book. There is a divine plan for marriage (279, 280, et al.), God's plan for humanity (383), and the *USCCA* is clear is saying that God has a "special plan" for each human being (63).

The popular pastor, Rick Warren, from Saddleback, California, has found success in using "God's Plan" in his blogs, picking up this term from his *The Purpose Driven Life: What on Earth Am I Here For?* With over thirty million copies of *The Purpose Driven Life* sold since its release in 2002, he has moved into children's books, including the following: *God's Big Plans for Me Storybook Bible: Based on the* New York Times *Bestseller* The Purpose Driven Life (2017).

And there are popular posts on Pastor Rick's devotional blog:

> God's Plan for Your Pain[41]
> God's Plan to Bring You to Heaven[42]
> God's Plans for You Started Before You Were Born[43]

It may be comforting to believe that God has a plan for you that started before you were born,[44] that it may involve a spouse, involves your pain, and eventually leads you to heaven. But we can also recognize that this is a drastic change from Old Testament passages that spoke only infrequently of God's plan for human beings, and then it was primarily that they follow Torah.

So, we can see the development of the term from Classical usage, to biblical, to Luke himself who applied "God's plan" to the events surrounding Jesus's life and death, including prophets before him and the Church after him. With such a convenient term to express what God had done in Jesus (i.e., fulfilled his own plan), later theologians and the Church itself applied and used the term widely and broadly. Nearly anything and everything could be understood as God's plan, including (unfortunately) slavery, but also states of life such as marriage, gender, or homosexuality, and how one is to behave in particular states of life or genders. The two passages from Isaiah and Jeremiah are cited often today by those preaching a prosperity gospel to the well-off and those who wish to be. But this is a far cry from the Old Testament, and even a far cry from what Luke had in mind about God's plan being fulfilled in Jesus. We might wonder what Luke the evangelist or Isaiah the prophet might think of Pastor Rick Warren's understanding of "God's plan for your pain."

Chapter Two

PROVIDENCE

To use the term *plan of God* necessarily involves a theistic, if not Christian or Jewish, worldview. But there is a broader, less strict term to speak of a more general, benevolent hand (metaphorically speaking) guiding events. Sometimes this is called "providence."

In antiquity, the Greek version of the popular travel writer Rick Steves was known as Strabo (63 BCE–24 CE). He wrote a well-known geography documenting many of the sites in the Mediterranean based on his own travels and what he had gleaned from outside sources.

In his book he describes the Plutonium (so named after Pluto, god of the underworld), a crevasse that seemed to lead into the depths of the earth. Misty vapors emanated from the opening. These "gates of hell," or gates to the underworld, were in the ancient city of Hierapolis, in modern Turkey, where there were also natural springs. The Plutonium was attended to by eunuch priests of the Great Mother of the gods, known as the Galli. Any living thing that approached the Plutonium would die, except for the Galli. Even bulls brought into the cave died. Strabo himself says he tossed sparrows in and they too died. After witnessing the Galli enter briefly into the cavern, Strabo wondered whether the Galli simply held their breath as he could see, or perhaps they were protected from the vapor because they were eunuchs, or possibly "divine providence."[1]

Pliny the Elder also mentions the deadly vapors in Hierapolis.[2] Like Strabo, Pliny says that no one could enter safely except the priests of the Great Mother of the gods. In fact, only recently, in the past decade, modern scientists conducted a study of the Plutonium and found that it was (still) emitting carbon dioxide.[3] In an ancient world without a modern understanding of CO_2, instruments with which to measure it, or even its effects on living animals, we can appreciate how this fissure in the earth became known as the "gates of hell." We might even appreciate Strabo's conjecture that the Galli were holding their breath, but they might also be protected from the vapors by Divine Providence or being eunuchs. When we do not comprehend something, it can be natural to refer to God, the gods, or Divine Providence, understood as that benevolent force that guides the world.

The word itself, *pro-vidence*, simply means "a foreseeing," though it has come to mean in English the foreseeing care and guidance of God or nature over the creatures of the earth. Sometimes it can mean "God," especially conceived of as an omniscient and wise benevolent force. Though providence can merely indicate a manifestation of divine care or direction of earthly activities, it is also closely related to the idea of God's plan. In that way it is understood as noted above in Cicero's work, as the "the foreknowledge and foretelling of events that happen by chance." Aside from Cicero, many other ancient authors wrote on the topic, including Seneca (*On Providence*) and Philo (*On Providence*).

CLASSICAL WORLD

The concept of *"providence"* has its roots in the classical world. Plato (ca. 424–ca. 348 BCE) himself says in *The Republic*,

As to the one who is loved by the gods, did we not agree that all that comes from the gods is the best possible…? …Similarly then as regards the just man, whether he becomes poor, or falls ill, or suffers any other of those things that seem evil, we must so take it that these things will end up in something good for him while he lives, or when he dies.[4]

The Greek historian Dionysius of Halicarnassus (ca. 60–ca. 7 BCE) wrote *Roman Antiquities* after moving to Rome, studying Latin, and reading Roman history. His multivolume work starts with the prehistory of the founding of the city by Romulus. Throughout the work, Dionysius speaks of how providence protected Rome and continued to protect it to his day.[5]

Not only does providence protect Rome, but it seems to favor Rome in battles. During the siege of Jerusalem by the Romans led by Titus around 70 CE, amid a fire that threatened to engulf the Romans and their siege engines, Josephus tells us,

Now, at the very beginning of this fire, a north wind that then blew proved terrible to the Romans; for by bringing the flame downward, it drove it upon them, and they were almost in despair of success, as fearing their machines would be burnt: but after this, on a sudden the wind changed into the south, as if it were done by Divine Providence, and blew strongly the contrary way, and carried the flame, and drove it against the wall, which was now on fire through its entire thickness. So the Romans, having now assistance from God, returned to their camp with joy, and resolved to attack their enemies the very next day; on which occasion they set their watch more carefully that night, lest any of the Jews should run away from them without being discovered.[6]

BIBLE

For human beings seeking security and comfort, it is often not enough for the divine merely to have foresight, as the word *providence* implies. Instead, many people want the divine to have care, guidance, and direction. The psalms provide such comfort, for example, in these verses addressed to God:

The eyes of all look to you,
and you give them their food in due season.
You open your hand,
satisfying the desire of every living thing.
(Ps 145:15–16)[7]

This attitude is reflected in the teaching of Jesus when he says, "Look at the birds of the air; they neither sow nor reap nor gather into barns, and yet your heavenly Father feeds them. Are you not of more value than they?" (Matt 6:26; see also Luke 12:24). It can be comforting to believe that actions in the world are guided by providence, a beneficial force for good.

In the same Gospel of Matthew, Jesus says, "Are not two sparrows sold for a penny? Yet not one of them will fall to the ground apart from your Father. And even the hairs of your head are all counted. So do not be afraid; you are of more value than many sparrows" (Matt 10:29–31; see also Luke 12:6–7).

Those Christians who are fond of such ideas also quote the apostle Paul, for in his letter to the Romans he writes, "We know that all things work together for good for those who love God, who are called according to his purpose" (Rom 8:28). And some ancient manuscripts go even further, as they read "God" as the subject of the verb, rendering the passage: "We know that God makes everything work for good for those who love God...."[8]

There are many passages in the Bible that speak to this mindset that God looks out for those who love him or even for all creation. And these scriptures support many modern preachers who are eager to tell their parishioners and church-goers that God's providential care looks out for them too.

EARLY AMERICAN HISTORY

Centuries after the Bible, many of the Puritans who set-tled in North America were motivated by a belief in Divine Providence. Scholars now refer to this movement as "Provi-dentialism," rooted in the theological notions of the Protestant reformer John Calvin (1509–64). The settlers believed that they had been chosen by God. We might wonder what the native peoples of the time would have said in response.

Providence was used in some of the foundational docu-ments of the United States. For example, the Declaration of Independence, written principally by Thomas Jefferson (1743–1826), concludes with the following words: "And for the sup-port of this Declaration, with a firm reliance on the protection of divine Providence, we mutually pledge to each other our Lives, our Fortunes and our sacred Honor."[9] The meaning of "divine Providence" in the Declaration of Independence has been the subject of much debate. Moreover, the term itself seems to have been added not by Jefferson but by the Conti-nental Congress.[10]

Not only was Thomas Jefferson the principal author of the Declaration of Independence, he also served as governor of Virginia, minister to France, and the nation's first secretary of state, second vice president, and third president, serving two terms. In his first presidential inaugural address (1801) the term *providence* also appears:

> Let us then, with courage and confidence, pur-sue our own federal and republican principles....

enlightened by a benign religion, professed indeed and practiced in various forms, yet all of them inculcating honesty, truth, temperance, gratitude and the love of man, acknowledging and adoring an overruling providence, which by all its dispensations proves that it delights in the happiness of man here, and his greater happiness hereafter; with all these blessings, what more is necessary to make us a happy and a prosperous people?[11]

Four years later, after his reelection and after the infamous Louisiana purchase, which doubled the size of the young country and itself contributed to the notion of manifest destiny in 1845,[12] Jefferson delivered his second inaugural in which he again invoked providence, this time in his concluding paragraph.

I shall now enter on the duties to which my fellow-citizens have again called me....I shall need too the favor of that being in whose hands we are: who led our fathers, as Israel of old, from their native land; and planted them in a country flowing with all the necessaries & comforts of life; who has covered our infancy with his providence, & our riper years with his wisdom & power: & to whose goodness I ask you to join in supplications with me, that he will so enlighten the minds of your servants, guide their councils, & prosper their measures, that whatsoever they do shall result in your good, & shall secure to you the peace, friendship, & approbation of all nations.[13]

The assumption that the United States was guided by providence has been a recurring theme throughout the nation's history, invoked by leaders of various political persuasions. Such a claim is certainly open to critique as well, as native Americans, slaves, undocumented immigrants, and others will testify.

In critical moments throughout United States history, providence seems to be especially invoked. For example, during the Civil War, when brother fought brother and hundreds of thousands were wounded or killed, Lincoln struggled to find a worthy and adequate general. When Ulysses S. Grant was promoted to lieutenant general by President Lincoln, Grant said,

> With the aid of the noble armies that have fought on so many fields for our common country, it will be my earnest endeavor not to disappoint your expectations. I feel the full weight of the responsibilities now devolving on me and know that if they are met it will be due to those armies, and above all to the favor of that Providence which leads both Nations and men.[14]

Lincoln himself invoked providence on March 4, 1865, in his second inaugural address, which is carved into the walls of his memorial in Washington. After years of war, now punctuated by his reelection, Lincoln pondered the role of the divine in the mighty struggle of North and South. His words may sound as much like an enlightened theologian as an American President:

> Both [North and South] read the same Bible and pray to the same God, and each invokes His aid against the other. It may seem strange that any men should dare to ask a just God's assistance in wringing their bread from the sweat of other men's faces, but let us judge not, that we be not judged. The prayers of both could not be answered. That of

neither has been answered fully. The Almighty has His own purposes. "Woe unto the world because of offenses; for it must needs be that offenses come, but woe to that man by whom the offense cometh" [Matt 18:7]. If we shall suppose that American slavery is one of those offenses which, in the providence of God, must needs come, but which, having continued through His appointed time, He now wills to remove, and that He gives to both North and South this terrible war as the woe due to those by whom the offense came, shall we discern therein any departure from those divine attributes which the believers in a living God always ascribe to Him? Fondly do we hope, fervently do we pray, that this mighty scourge of war may speedily pass away. Yet, if God wills that it continue until all the wealth piled by the bondsman's two hundred and fifty years of unrequited toil shall be sunk, and until every drop of blood drawn with the lash shall be paid by another drawn with the sword, as was said three thousand years ago, so still it must be said "the judgments of the Lord are true and righteous altogether" [Ps 19:9].

With malice toward none, with charity for all, with firmness in the right as God gives us to see the right, let us strive on to finish the work we are in, to bind up the nation's wounds, to care for him who shall have borne the battle and for his widow and his orphan, to do all which may achieve and cherish a just and lasting peace among ourselves and with all nations.[15]

But not only heroes of the past appeal to providence. Many might be surprised to learn that some of the most heinous and destructive persons from history attributed their power and success to providence as well. There is no better example of this than Adolf Hitler.

WORLD WAR II

Not even four years after becoming Chancellor of Germany in 1933, Hitler violated the Treaty of Versailles by reoccupying the Rhineland in the face of inaction by the British, French, and other allies. He said, "I go the way that Providence dictates with the assurance of a sleepwalker."[16] His gambit was successful. When many others might have folded in the face of pressure, Hitler stood firm and interpreted his success as due to providence. Hitler had the audacity to push the issue of the Rhineland occupation, sensing that the nations who were victorious after World War I were reluctant to fight another war, and attributing his own success to providence and even destiny.[17]

To commemorate his four years in office, Hitler spoke to the Reichstag on January 30, 1937, saying, "Today I must humbly thank Providence whose grace has enabled me, once an unknown soldier in the war, to bring to a successful issue the struggle for our honor and rights as a nation."[18] When asked in 1939 why he didn't travel with more protection other than one or two bodyguards, Hitler "replied that a man must have faith in Providence, then slapped his trouser pocket. 'See, I always carry a pistol but even that would be useless. If my end is decided, only this will protect me.'"[19]

The more powerful Hitler and the German nation grew, the more he and others believed that providence was guiding his success. After annexing Austria in the Anschluss, Hitler spoke to the fascist chancellor of Austria, Kurt Schuschnigg, and said, "I have a historic mission; and this mission I will fulfill because

Providence has destined me to do so. I thoroughly believe in this mission; it is my life."[20]

Not everyone was sure that Hitler was carrying out God's will. In fact, there were several assassination attempts against him. But when these failed, "The Catholic Press throughout the Reich piously declared that it was the miraculous working of Providence which had protected the Führer. Cardinal Faulhaber [Archbishop of Munich from 1917–52] sent a telegram and instructed that a Te Deum be sung in the cathedral of Munich, 'to thank Divine Providence in the name of the archdiocese for the Führer's fortunate escape.'"[21]

Hitler believed he was carrying out God's will, that he reported to a higher being. After Hitler fired a general who would not carry out his orders, Hitler said to him, "I, myself, for instance, am not in a position to go to my superior, God Almighty, and say to Him, 'I am not going on with it, because I don't want to take the responsibility.'"[22]

In November 1941, prior to outbreak of war with the United States, Hitler said, "No power can shake the German Reich now. Divine Providence has willed it that I carry the fulfillment of a Germanic task."[23] By 1944, Nazi Germany was being encircled and closed in on from all directions. During the summer of 1944 in Germany, after the Allied invasion of Normandy, some of Hitler's entourage believed the war effort was lost, and that they were being led by a madman who would stop at nothing, even the eventual ruination of Germany. These officers and others made a daring pact to assassinate Hitler and to launch a coup. These events were dramatized in the 2008 motion picture *Valkyrie*.

In sum, the German officer Claus von Stauffenberg led an effort to place a briefcase bomb next to Hitler during a meeting in the Wolf's Lair, one of Hitler's headquarters. The initial plan to have the bomb detonate in an enclosed room to maximize damage had to be altered when, on July 20, 1944, Hitler moved the meeting to another room due to the summer heat. Windows were opened to facilitate a nonexistent breeze. Officers were with Hitler poring over maps laid out on a narrow, heavy oak table. Stauffenberg positioned the bomb-bearing briefcase only six feet from Hitler, leaning on the inside of one of the heavy oak table supports, before excusing himself from the meeting. Minutes later, upon seeing the explosion from a distance, Stauffenberg was convinced Hitler had been killed. The coup was underway. But unknown to him, Hitler survived!

Shortly after Stauffenberg had excused himself from the meeting, an aide attempted to get a closer look at the maps when the briefcase obstructed him. The aide simply moved the briefcase to the outside of the table support, a fleeting act that effectively saved Hitler's life.

In a radio speech broadcast throughout the country in the early hours of the next morning, Hitler said, "I was spared a fate which held no horror for me, but would have had terrible consequences for the German people. I see in it a sign from Providence that I must, and therefore shall, continue my work."[24] Many German citizens agreed that providence had saved their Führer. Many of the seditionists, including Stauffenberg, had in that brief time already been rounded up and shot. Many thousands more would share their fate.

So many small, insignificant decisions came together to spare Hitler. The meeting was not in a concrete bunker where the explosion would have certainly killed him, but had been moved to a room with open windows. Hitler himself was standing in front of a door that led to a long narrow hallway, where the main force of the explosion travelled. Most significantly, the briefcase had been placed on the inside of the table support, but was moved at the last minute to the outside of the support. For Hitler, this escape from a well-planned assassination attempt was providential.[25]

The day after the assassination attempt Hitler said to some wounded officers, "Don't you agree that I should consider it a sign of Fate that it intends to preserve me for my assigned task?" His survival "only confirmed the conviction that Almighty God has called me to lead the German people— not to final defeat but to victory."[26]

At 4:00 a.m., less than twenty-four hours after the assassination attempt, Minister of Propaganda Goebbels recognized that if Hitler had been killed it would have been understood as God's judgment. He said to Himmler, the leader of the SS, "For in history only facts speak as evidence. And they are this time on our side."[27]

There were earlier thwarted attempts to assassinate Hitler and others that went awry. Having survived an assassination attempt in late 1939, Hitler said, "Now I am completely content! The fact that I left the Burgerbraukeller earlier than usual is a corroboration of Providence's intention to let me reach my goal."[28] March 1943 saw two other unsuccessful assassination attempts,[29] and there were other failed plots later as well.[30]

The example of Hitler is included merely to demonstrate how providence can be and often is invoked to buttress a point of view or action, even the most horrendous. Even the Archbishop of Munich saw providence at work when assassination attempts were foiled. Simply claiming that something is providential is by no means surety of the claim. And as we saw, God's plan, will, and providence have been used to maintain the status quo. As Goebbels said, "in history, only facts speak as evidence." There are countless examples throughout history and in our own times of those claiming Divine Providence for their fortune or fate, which itself is a concept closely linked to providence.

Chapter Three

DESTINY OR FATE

Nothing ever springs miraculously out of
nothing. The fact is that all mortals are
in the grip of fear, because they observe
many things happening on earth and in
the sky and, being at a complete loss for an
explanation of their cause, suppose that a
supernatural power is responsible for them.
Therefore, as soon as we have seen that
nothing can be created out of nothing, we
shall have a clearer view of the object of
our search, namely the explanation of the
source of all created things and of the way
in which all things happen independently of
the gods.

—Lucretius, *On the Nature of Things*, 1.151–59

The 1985 blockbuster movie *Back to the Future* depicts what
happens if one were able to travel back in time to alter events.
In the film, Marty McFly, played by Michael J. Fox, travels
back from 1985 to 1955 and accidentally interrupts the
occasion when his father, George (played by Crispin Glover),
and mother, Lorraine (played by Lea Thompson), meet as

teenagers. Most of the movie is then Marty trying to (re) connect George and Lorraine. At one point, Marty convinces George to tell Lorraine that he is her destiny, but George trips over the word and claims that he is her "density."

Gwyneth Paltrow starred in a 1990s movie, *Sliding Doors*, which begins with one story and diverges into two, based on whether the main character catches a subway or narrowly misses it as the doors close (thus the title *Sliding Doors*). Two story lines are then followed independently as the audience sees what her life becomes in each. Just when the audience might think that one story line is better, tragedy strikes, and the other story line seems preferable. This back and forth happens throughout the film, toying with the viewer who might want to settle on which result is "better" for the main character. Audiences might contemplate that what appears to be "good" might not actually be. Challenges that one faces can lead to better results, even if this is not fully comprehended at the time.

Another film, less popular but more recent than either *Back to the Future* or *Sliding Doors*, *The Adjustment Bureau*, also explores the role of destiny.[1] When the main character, played by Matt Damon, reconnects with another who could become the "love of his life," he is confronted by men in business suits who claim, "We are the guys who keep everything going according to plan." Later they say again, "We are here to keep you on plan." Matt Damon's character asks, "Are you an angel?" and the reply comes, "We've been called that. We are like case officers." They claim to work for, "The Chairman" but "you have other names for him." These case officers are known as the adjustment team, creating small changes that might ordinarily be perceived as "normal" events (a mobile call failure, a sprained ankle, a narrowly missed taxi or bus), but these events all happen to keep things moving according to a plan.

As this is a movie, the adjustments that the adjustment team needs to make become greater and greater throughout the course of the film, leading to a confrontation with Matt Damon's character who is told, "You can't outrun your fate," by which they mean he should not be with the woman. But he replies, "All I have are the choices I make, and I choose her." In the end, he is with the woman and is told by the adjustment team, "What happened was a serious deviation from the plan. So, the chairman rewrote it." The closing words of the movie are spoken by a member of the adjustment team to the Matt Damon character, but are certainly meant for the audience:

> Most people live life on the path we set for them, too afraid to explore any other. But once in a while people like you come along who knock down all the obstacles we put in your way. People who realize free will is a gift you'll never know how to use until you fight for it. I think that's the chairman's real plan, that maybe someday we won't write the plan; you will.

The movie and the short story on which it is based encourage the audience and the readers to recognize the role of free will for each individual human being. It's not enough to simply follow life's path without questioning one's own purpose, desires, and goals. What may *appear* to be an external "plan" can be altered by our own choices.

In and apart from the movies, *destiny* and *fate* are two terms that are often interwoven. Each refers to events that happen or must happen due to some preordained succession. Often, especially when fate is concerned, these predetermined or foreordained events may be presaged or preceded by still other actions that are called oracles, signs, omens, or portents. In many respects, destiny and fate function in a way similar to providence,[2] though often without a notion of the divine.

We saw above that Hitler considered himself a child of Fate,[3] and that after he survived the bombing assassination attempt in July 1944, he said with a smile to his secretaries, "Well, my ladies, once again everything has turned out well for me. More proof that Fate has selected me for my mission. Otherwise I wouldn't be alive."[4]

> "One must listen to an inner voice and believe in one's fate. And I believe very deeply that destiny has selected me for the German nation. So long as I am needed by the people, so long as I am responsible for the life of the Reich, I shall live." He pictured himself as another Christ. "And when I am no longer needed, after my mission is accomplished, then I shall be called away."[5]

In Ancient Greek, the terms that mean "fate" can also mean "share" or "portion" (*moira, aisa, moros, morsimos, heimartai*). Homer speaks of one's share falling to one at birth (*Iliad* 20.128; 24.209–10; *Odyssey* 7.198). "And the most certain fate of each human person is death, and the gods are powerless to save one from that fate" (*Odyssey* 3.236–8). Fate is a theme throughout Homer, and it usually means the orderly sequence of a plot or determined events. Yet there were occasions when this plot could be disrupted, for example, when the Cyclops eats his guests, it is not in accordance with fate (*kata moiran*) (*Odyssey* 9.352).[6]

The Latin term *fatus* is the etymological basis for the English term *fate*. *Fatus* comes from the term *fari*, "to speak." Thus, *fatus* could mean an oracle or saying, which we will explore in more detail below. Cicero, the orator who gave us *De Divinatione*, quoted above, spoke of fate as the orderly succession of causes (*De Divinatione* 1.125). After composing *De Divinatione*, Cicero also wrote *De Fato*. For the Stoics, according to Cicero, "all things happen by fate" (*De Fato* 15.33). The concept of "fate" was variously defined in antiquity but often equated with providence or the role of Zeus (e.g., Seneca, *De Beneficiis* 4.7.2).

Josephus too mentions fate several times in his *Antiquities*. In one passage he defines it thusly: "We are persuaded that human actions are thereby determined beforehand by an inevitable necessity, and we call her Fate, because there is nothing which is not done by her."[7]

We recall that during the siege of Jotapata, Josephus was spared the death pact that he helped forge. In that telling, he wondered if that happened by chance or providence (*Wars of the Jews* 3.387–392), or perhaps it was his own cunning! What he says in *Antiquities* might lead us to believe that fate could have had a hand in that fortuitous event too.

The Church fathers discussed fate as well and dismissed the idea that fate controlled human lives. Instead, someone like Justin Martyr (ca. 100–ca. 165 CE) said human beings have free will (2 Apol 7; see also 1 Apol 44). Another early Christian thinker, Tatian (ca. 120–ca. 80 CE), also favors free will over a predetermined fate (Address to the Greeks, 7, 9, 11).

Though "free will" might be official Catholic Church teaching, with its roots in Scripture and the fathers, many modern people consider destiny or fate to be a meaningful idea by which to interpret events. It's even said that Ulysses S. Grant "had a clever way of placing himself in the pathway to success, then calling it fate."[8]

Or consider the words of Winston Churchill, who on May 10, 1940, was appointed prime minister in large part because Lord Halifax (the preferred candidate among many elites) declined. Though Churchill had had his eyes on the role for years, it had always seemed out of reach. Now at sixty-five he had attained the office on the cusp of a momentous time in world history. He later wrote of the experience: "I felt as I were walking with Destiny, and that all my past life had been but a preparation for this hour and for this trial....I was sure I should not fail."[9]

ANCIENT ORACLES

Though few people believe in or consult oracles today, the most famous in antiquity was the Delphic oracle, also known as the oracle of Apollo. In ancient times, generals, politicians, and others often would consult the oracle to gain insight into the outcome of a major decision.[10] The result of consulting the oracle was necessarily ambiguous, for it was believed that the signs of the gods combined with human interpretation did not allow for entirely accurate certainty. The ancients believed that there were limits to what human beings could know about the future, even if the gods themselves knew. Thus, human fallibility and shortcomings might misinterpret the message or perceive it only slightly. Even the process of consulting the oracle seems to have been designed to accommodate this fallibility.

At Delphi, a priestess known as the Pythia (a chaste female diviner who served in that role for life), "received the spirit" (*pneuma*). The ancient Greek travel writer Strabo, whom we have met before in these pages, describes the process by which the Pythia receives the spirit: "They say that the oracular [source] is at a deep hollow cave, which has not a very wide opening. From this cave a spirit of ecstatic divine inspiration proceeds. There is a tripod situated high over the mouth of the cave, which the Pythia mounts, and, once receiving the spirit, utters oracles in meter and in verse."[11] The uttered oracles were then interpreted and written down by the prophets and priests of Apollo who shared the message with the one who had requested it.

Croesus, King of Lydia

Delphi was not the only place or temple to have an oracle. Herodotus (ca. 484–ca. 425 BCE), often referred to as the "father of history" as he was the first to write an orderly and systematic narration of events past, tells us that Croesus, king of Lydia, who reigned from 560–546 BCE, wanted to test the accuracy of oracles. At that time, the Kingdom of Lydia was roughly the western half of Asia Minor, modern-day Turkey. Croesus sent his servants from Sardis, the capital city of Lydia, to consult many various oracles and to bring back what they said. Here is how Herodotus describes it:

> And when he sent to test these shrines he gave the Lydians these instructions: they were to keep track of the time from the day they left Sardis, and on the hundredth day inquire of the oracles what Croesus, king of Lydia, son of Alyattes, was doing then; then they were to write down whatever the oracles answered and bring the reports back to him.[12]

The Pythian priestess (from the oracle at Delphi) said this on the one hundredth day:

> I know the number of the grains of sand and the
> extent of the sea,
> And understand the mute and hear the voiceless.
> The smell has come to my senses of a strong-
> shelled tortoise
> Boiling in a cauldron together with a lamb's flesh,
> Under which is bronze and over which is bronze.[13]

When Croesus read that phrase from Delphi, he was astonished as he had on that one hundredth day cut up a tortoise and

36

a lamb and boiled them together in a bronze cauldron with a bronze lid.[14] The other oracles did not measure up when compared to what the Pythian priestess had uttered. Croesus thereafter made great sacrifices to the god of Delphi, had fashioned a gold lion weighing ten talents (nearly six hundred pounds) to be placed at the temple in Delphi, along with many other gifts and offerings. Clearly, he was impressed, and he believed that this oracle was the authentic one.

Croesus was also concerned about the Persians and was looking for a way to keep them in check. So when his servants delivered his gifts and tributes to the temple at Delphi, he asked them to consult the oracle again, this time, concerning whether he ought to attack the Persians by himself or with allies. The oracle said, "If he should send an army against the Persians he would destroy a great empire. And they advised him to discover the mightiest of the Greeks and make them his friends."[15] So Croesus allied himself with Sparta and set out to defeat the Persians. But the great empire Croesus destroyed was his own. Cyrus the Persian king captured Lydia and Croesus himself. The kingdom of Lydia would now be part of the Persian Empire. The ambiguity of the oracle could devastate mighty kings.

The Battle of Salamis

There is another famous example of the Delphic oracle being consulted that stands out. In 480 BCE the dominant Persians, led now by Xerxes, had advanced to Greece and were preparing an invasion. The Greek city-states (Athens, Sparta, and others) banded together in alliance against the dominant Persians. Three hundred Spartans made a defensive stand at Thermopylae and held off the Persian advance for some time. This battle has been memorialized and popularized throughout history, including most recently in the 2007 motion picture *300*.

When the Athenians learned of the Spartan defeat, the Athenians consulted the oracle of Delphi. As told by the Greek historian Herodotus, the oracle stated, via a priestess by the name of Aristonice,

> Wretches, why do you linger here? Rather flee from
>   your houses and city,
> Flee to the ends of the earth from the circle
>   embattled of Athens!
> The head will not remain in its place, nor in the
>   body,
> Nor the feet beneath, nor the hands, nor the parts
>   between;
> But all is ruined, for fire and the headlong god of war
>   speeding in a Syrian chariot will bring you low.
> Many a fortress too, not yours alone, will he
>   shatter;
> Many a shrine of the gods will he give to the flame
>   for devouring;
> Sweating for fear they stand, and quaking for dread
>   of the enemy,
> Running with gore are their roofs, foreseeing the
>   stress of their sorrow;
> Therefore I bid you depart from the sanctuary.
> Have courage to lighten your evil.[16]

A message like that had little ambiguity and spelled doom for the Athenians. So, they asked for another! This second time the oracle stated,

> Vainly does Pallas strive to appease great Zeus of
>   Olympus;
> Words of entreaty are vain, and so too cunning
>   counsels of wisdom.

Nevertheless I will speak to you again of strength
adamantine.
All will be taken and lost that the sacred border of
Cecrops
Holds in keeping today, and the dales divine of
Cithaeron;
Yet a wood-built wall will by Zeus all-seeing be
granted
To the Trito-born, a stronghold for you and your
children.
Await not the host of horse and foot coming
from Asia,
Nor be still, but turn your back and withdraw from
the foe.
Truly a day will come when you will meet him face
to face.
Divine Salamis, you will bring death to women's
sons
When the corn is scattered, or the harvest
gathered in.[17]

This second message, like the first, portended doom as
well. But there was seemed to be a glimmer of hope. The key
term in the second oracle was the "wooden wall" that would
be a stronghold for the Greek city-states and their children.
What precisely did that mean? Some considered it to be the
thorn bushes that surrounded the Acropolis (the highest point
in Athens where the temple of Athena stood). The famous
Athenian Themistocles (524–459 BCE), who had fought at the
Battle of Marathon, had another answer. He postulated that
the wooden wall was their fleet of ships. Having convinced the
inhabitants of his interpretation, he then convinced the Athenians to abandon their city to save themselves. The Greek navy
defeated the Persians at the Battle of Salamis, after which the

Persians retreated. In fact, that could be said to be the high point of the Persian advance.

Socrates

Of the most famous oracles from Delphi, one about the philosopher Socrates (ca. 470–399 BCE) is paramount. Socrates's friend Chaerephon asked the oracle whether there was anyone in Athens wiser than Socrates. The oracle replied, "No one." Socrates was incredulous, thinking to himself, "What in the world does the god mean, and what riddle is he propounding? For I am conscious that I am not wise either much or little. What then does he mean by declaring that I am the wisest? He certainly cannot be lying, for that is not possible for him."[18]

Socrates proceeded on his quest to investigate the meaning of the oracle. But after seeking anyone who was wiser, Socrates admitted that the oracle was correct, only because human wisdom is nothing and he acknowledges that he is ignorant, whereas others who lack knowledge remain adamant in claiming knowledge.[19] Socrates summed it up like this:

> I am wiser than this man; for neither of us really
> knows anything fine and good, but this man thinks
> he knows something when he does not, whereas I,
> as I do not know anything, do not think I do either.
> I seem, then, in just this little thing to be wiser than
> this man at any rate, that what I do not know I do
> not think I know either.[20]

Among other things, Socrates's quest brought upon him the ire of the learned because he made the lesser argument the stronger, and he was said to corrupt the young. On these charges he was found guilty and put to death. Though Socrates himself does not seem to have written anything, certainly not anything extant, his pupil Plato made up for that, writing dialogues espousing his philosophy. Plato's own disciple Aristotle (384–322 BCE) took a different tack from Plato, and together the two of them represent two broad and distinct branches of Greek philosophy. Aristotle himself was hired as a tutor to Alexander, son of King Philip of Macedon. This Alexander became known as "the Great," for by the time he was thirty-three he had led armies and conquered the eastern Mediterranean, Persia, and Asia (modern-day India and Afghanistan) where he died.

Alexander the Great

Alexander the Great (356–323 BCE) attempted to consult the oracle before he moved against Asia. But he arrived in Delphi on a day when it was not considered lawful to consult the oracle. Not accepting this refusal, Alexander took hold of the Pythia herself and, despite her protestations, began to drag her to the temple. She replied, "You are invincible, my son!" Alexander let her go, saying he had the oracle he wanted![21]

We can see how influential and important oracles, particularly the Delphic oracle, were in antiquity. Even so, the ancient historian Polybius (200–118 BCE) maintained that many clever leaders cloaked their actions in the mantle of divine providence or oracular support so the populace would embrace their programs more fully.[22]

Chapter Four

SIGNS AND OMENS

The Delphic oracle was a means used by the ancients to determine what the future might hold. As noted previously, the ancient Greeks believed that the gods knew the future, but there would or could be some translation difficulties when humans consulted the gods. Even so, it was certainly possible to make this connection, however haphazard or ambiguous it might be.

As a corollary to the belief that the gods knew the future and that human beings could discern that future by consulting an oracle, there were signs indicating future events that could also be discerned. Not everyone had access to the Delphic or other oracles. So these signs were an important way for people to read the intentions of the gods or see through a window into the future. At least one ancient author proclaimed the superiority of oracles when compared to omens, so if omens were unclear, that was the time to consult an oracle.[1] Sometimes these signs or omens were preceded by dreams, visions, or premonitions if these were not the signs or omens themselves.

Ancient and modern people look for signs or omens to tell them how to discern meaning. Merriam-Webster's definition of *omen* is "an occurrence or phenomenon believed to portend a future event."[2] One does not need to believe that signs or omens come from the divine to believe in signs or omens themselves. There are many instances throughout history of human beings understanding different events to be signs, omens, or portents. We will consider some below.

The word *sign* with reference to the divine appears throughout popular culture today. In the best-selling *Hillbilly Elegy*, the author J. D. Vance tells his own story of his adoption by a surrogate father by the name of "Bob." As the author tells it,

> Eventually, Dad told me, he asked God for three signs that an adoption was in my best interest. Those signs apparently appeared, and I became the legal son of Bob, a man I'd known for barely a year. I don't doubt the truth of this account, and though I empathize with the obvious difficulty of the decision, I have never felt comfortable with the idea of leaving your child's fate to signs from God.[3]

For modern Christians, and especially those of a particular denominational bent, there is a special kind of sign that has its roots in the Bible. This sign is referred to as a "fleece."

FLEECE

One of the more prominent examples of a sign from God in the Bible would be the sign of the fleece from Judges 6. It has become even more popular now because of evangelical preachers. In the passage from Judges, we hear about Gideon, one of the twelve judges whose stories are told in the book, seeking confirmation from God prior to engaging in battle.

> Then Gideon said to God, "In order to see whether you will deliver Israel by my hand, as you have said, I am going to lay a fleece of wool on the threshing floor; if there is dew on the fleece alone, and it is

dry on all the ground, then I shall know that you will deliver Israel by my hand, as you have said." And it was so. When he rose early next morning and squeezed the fleece, he wrung enough dew from the fleece to fill a bowl with water. Then Gideon said to God, "Do not let your anger burn against me, let me speak one more time; let me, please, make trial with the fleece just once more; let it be dry only on the fleece, and on all the ground let there be dew." And God did so that night. It was dry on the fleece only, and on all the ground there was dew. (Judg 6:36–40)

At least one contemporary biblical commentator refers to this episode as resembling "the modern theater of the absurd."[4] The first instance of the fleece having absorbed the dew while the floor was dry is a natural phenomenon.[5] The second instance represents for the reader the confirmation that the sign is from God. The following chapter in Judges tells how Gideon (rather the LORD) won the battle, but not before Gideon follows additional instructions from God. The story of the fleece might be part of what fuels some modern notions of an Old Testament God who is himself rather testy, demanding, and even illogical. Instructions issued to human beings seem arbitrary so that human beings need ways to learn God's will in order not to offend but also to succeed.

Examples of modern Christians "putting out a fleece" to learn the will of the Lord and seek his direction are legion; here is only one example.

Several years ago, I had the worst year ever teaching school. I had fought the wiles of the devil long enough! I had reacted badly, not once but several times throughout that year. During the first semester I had some bad-to-the-bone children....

44

Later, in second semester, I had to teach a biology class of tenth graders who already knew more than I ever cared to know about biology. I don't think more than one student ever read an assignment all term. That class was held in the main building, a long hike from my main classroom; and I had to be in the classroom before they all arrived, or it would have been utter confusion! I had twenty-eight wild teenagers to control, trick into learning, and polish into fine young people. Teachers are supposed to do that, aren't they?

By the end of the term, I packed up my things so that I could move out during the summer. I was never going to be a teacher again. I went with my family to the beach (to make them as miserable as I was). While sitting on the balcony one morning reading my Bible at the place where we were staying, I made a deal with God. I was not haughty—just heartbroken and desperate. I told Him that if I were to continue teaching school, He would have to convince me that He had called me to be a teacher because right then I could not do it anymore.

I put out my fleece. I needed two students to write me a note, thanking me for helping them. Now, I live in a small town, and I frequently meet former and current students. That didn't count. They had to be letters, written and sent to me. That prayer was on a Saturday, and I had to have the letters by Wednesday of the next week!

On Monday, I received a note from Amy. She had frequently left sweet notes on my desk all year. I loved her so much, and I appreciated her note. The next day, I received a note from Yolonda, thanking me for recommending her for a job. She was a quiet

45

student, always doing her work and rarely saying anything to me.

God was so kind to this broken reed of a servant. He sent me not only one letter from Amy but also a second one from Yolonda. So I tearfully thanked Him for His graciousness to me and decided not to leave my place of service.

Since then, I have never sunk to that depth of discouragement. God has put me here, and when He changes His mind, He will notify me, just as He did Gideon. He delights in guiding His children.[6]

One sees in this example how a modern person appropriates the biblical story for herself. We wonder about what the other twenty-six students in her class thought!

In evangelical, or even broadly Christian popular theology, when one wants confirmation of a pending decision, one might "put out a fleece" and await confirmation. The fleece itself might be anything, as our distraught teacher in the story above shows. But for every example of a successful "fleece" there is likely at least one unsuccessful example. The following story is one such example.

Jessica had just moved to a new city when she joined a mom's group at the parish. Young mothers would come together once a week to share their lives, hopes, dreams, day-to-day struggles, and more. One young mother, Anne, announced to the group that she was pregnant. She and her husband already had two boys. The young couple thought this would be her last pregnancy, and they were hoping this new baby would be a girl. Anne asked the group to pray that they would have a girl.

Jessica was troubled by the request. It seemed natural to hope for a boy or a girl, but what if the family had a boy when they wanted a girl, or vice versa? Would the family be happy with a boy? These thoughts are common among young parents; anyone with children is familiar with the flurry of emotion, feelings, sentiments, and momentary thoughts that this experience can bring. Still, Jessica was concerned.

At the following week's meeting, Anne said to the group that she had decided how they would have a girl. Anne was going to make a novena (nine days of prayer) to St. Thérèse of Lisieux, also known as "the Little Flower." St. Thérèse (1873–97) was a young nun who died of tuberculosis at the age of twenty-four. Her autobiographical memoir was published after her death as *The Story of a Soul*, and it made her one of the most popular saints in the twentieth-century Church. She referred to herself as a "little flower" of Jesus, and she thought of the world as God's garden with each person being a flower.

This novena, this special prayer over a series of days would "work like a charm," according to Anne. She was not going to tell her husband but wanted everyone to pray this novena with her. On the last day of the novena, Anne excitedly called her friends to say that her husband had given her a rose that day for no apparent reason. Anne interpreted this as a sign from St. Thérèse, the Little Flower, that she would have a girl. With this knowledge Anne chose a name for the baby and painted the room pink. Later, Jessica heard how disappointed Anne was when she gave birth to a third boy. Anne reported back to the group that a girl was not in "God's plan."

It can be difficult to interpret meaning when putting out fleeces for God or even attempting to work through a saint. As we see from the example of Anne, merely wanting something badly enough, even when we experience a sign, is not sufficient. Something more is certainly at work.

SIGNS (FROM GOD)

To make light of signs sent by the gods
is nothing less than to disbelieve in the
existence of the gods.

—Cicero, *De Divinatione*, I.46

We would be wrong to think that only those in the ancient world discerned the hand of god(s) in daily events. A fascinating example of such a case comes from the former top theological enforcer for the United States Conference of Catholic Bishops (USCCB), Fr. Thomas Weinandy, OFM Cap. Fr. Weinandy, who holds a doctorate in historical theology, might be said to be aligned with Pope Benedict XVI and the cultural warrior bishops in the United States. From 2005 to early 2013 he served as executive director of the Secretariat for Doctrine and Pastoral Practices at the USCCB. He was an advisor to the USCCB after that. During his time as executive director he wrote critically of theologians in the United States such as Elizabeth Johnson, issuing public rebukes of no less than five of them. Coming from a place of professional and academic training in the realm of theology, as top enforcer for the U.S. Bishops he was apparently comfortable critiquing some of the leading theologians in the country. In 2013 he even received an award from Pope Francis, and the following year Pope Francis appointed him to the International Theological Commission for a standard five-year term.

This background is what makes the next story so bizarre. After the election of Jorge Bergoglio as Pope Francis, and in his subsequent dealings with him, Fr. Weinandy eventually had several concerns about the Pope's own theology. Not one to take such concerns lightly, Fr. Weinandy prayed about this a great deal before sending a letter to the Pope in 2017 in which he wrote that "a chronic confusion seems to mark your pontificate." After not receiving an answer for several months, Fr. Weinandy released his letter publicly. Shortly thereafter, Fr. Weinandy resigned from his position as advisor at the USCCB.[7]

Fr. Weinandy was asked why he wrote and then released such a letter critical of the Pope's theology. He said that he prayed about the decision. He prayed about the state of the Church, his own anxieties, and whether he ought to write to the Pope himself. Fr. Weinandy could no longer sleep. And from here we hear the story in his own voice:

At 1:15 AM I got up and went outside for short time. When I went back to my room, I said to the Lord: "If you want me to write something, you have to give me a clear sign. This is what the sign must be. Tomorrow morning I am going to Saint Mary Major's to pray and then I am going to Saint John Lateran. After that I am coming back to Saint Peter's to have lunch with a seminary friend of mine. During that interval, I must meet someone that I know but have not seen in a very long time and would never expect to see in Rome at this time. That person cannot be from the United States, Canada or Great Britain. Moreover, that person has to say to me in the course of our conversation, 'Keep up the good writing.'"

The next morning I did all of the above and by the time I met my seminarian friend for lunch what I had asked the Lord the following night was no longer in the forefront of my mind. However, towards the end of the meal an archbishop appeared between two parked cars right in front of our table (we were sitting outside). I had not seen him for over twenty years, long before he became an archbishop. We recognized one another immediately. What made his appearance even more unusual was that because of his recent personal circumstances I would never have expected to see him in Rome or anywhere else, other than in his own archdiocese. (He was from none of the above mentioned countries.) We spoke about his coming to Rome and caught up on what we were doing. I then introduced him to my seminarian friend. He said to my friend that we had met a long time ago and that he had, at that time, just finished reading my book on the immutability of God and the Incarnation. He told my friend that it was an excellent book, that it helped him sort out the issue, and that my friend should read the book. Then he turned to me and said: "Keep up the good writing."[8]

Fr. Weinandy continues and expresses his amazement that his demanding sign was fulfilled by an archbishop no less. Clearly, the fulfillment of this sign was especially meaningful for Fr. Weinandy, and he acted because of it. But perhaps more amazing is that Fr. Weinandy is a professional, academically trained theologian who, backed by the USCCB, had critiqued other theologians for their apparent missteps and shortcomings. Yet, his religiosity and "meaning-making" of signs is rather pedestrian. That is, his theological sophistication sounds in the letter much like anyone who throws out a "fleece." For all his academic training, Fr. Weinandy sounds remarkably like anyone else in the pew, only his prayers were said at St. Peter's Basilica in Rome, and the demanding sign that he put forth was fulfilled by an archbishop. And all of this for Fr. Weinandy was about critiquing Pope Francis's theology!

Just as priests look for signs from God before they go about their work (even criticizing the Pope), other, more nefarious characters seek signs from God too. Adolf Hitler became chancellor of Germany in January 1933. About four weeks later, on February 27, 1933, the Reichstag (German Parliament building) burned to the ground. At the time, and even now, the origins of the fire were unclear. But the Nazi party used that event to consolidate power and suspend freedom of assembly, speech, press, and other liberties, in what became known as the Reichstag Fire Decree. But at the time, in February 1933, the burning of the Reichstag was seen by Hitler's supporters as a sign from God; others saw it as the work of communists.[9] Whether or not the fire was the work of communists or set by members of the Nazi party to frame others, it became a convenient tool for disassembling the fledgling German democracy. As a result of the Reichstag Fire Decree, civil liberties were suspended and never restored again under the Nazi regime. Signs from God are in the eye of the beholder.

OMEN

A favorable omen corresponds to the will of the gods.

—Dionysius of Halicarnassus,
Roman Antiquities, 2.6.3

Aside from fleeces in the biblical world, or signs from God interpreted by believers and nonbelievers alike, the ancient Greek and Roman world also discerned the meaning of omens, closely related to the concept of signs. The philosopher and biographer Plutarch (ca. 46–ca. 119 CE) was also a priest of the Temple of Apollo at Delphi. He eventually became a Roman citizen and wrote a work entitled *Illustrious Lives*. In that work Plutarch mentions a sign from heaven presaging Alexander the Great's victory in Asia. One such omen was a cypress-wood statue of Orpheus (a legendary poet, prophet, and musician from ancient Greek mythology) that was at Leibethra (a Greek city at the foot of Mount Olympus). This wooden statue was said to have sweated. Many feared the sign, but Alexander took a contrarian view, saying it foretold his victories "worthy of song and story, which would cost poets and musicians much toil and sweat to celebrate."[10]

Still, we would be wise to remember that not all ancients shared this predilection for signs. For example, Cicero says, "There is, then, no statement less worthy of a natural philosopher than that anything can be foretold with a certainty by uncertain signs."[11] But more than a century later, the Roman historian Suetonius (69–122 CE), himself a rather superstitious character, tells us that there were many signs presaging the assassination of Julius Caesar (100–44 BCE). We hear Suetonius now in his own words:

> Now Caesar's approaching murder was foretold to him by unmistakable signs. A few months before, when the settlers assigned to the colony at Capua by the Julian Law were demolishing some tombs of great antiquity, to build country houses, and plied their work with the greater vigor because as they rummaged about they found a quantity of vases of ancient workmanship, there was discovered in a tomb, which was said to be that of Capys, the founder of Capua, a bronze tablet, inscribed with Greek words and characters to this purport: "Whenever the bones of Capys shall be moved, it will come to pass that a son of Ilium shall be slain at the hands of his kindred, and presently avenged at heavy cost to Italy." And let no one think this tale a myth or a lie, for it is vouched for by Cornelius Balbus, an intimate friend of Caesar. Shortly before his death, as he was told, the herds of horses which he had dedicated to the river Rubicon when he crossed it, and had let loose without a keeper,

stubbornly refused to graze and wept copiously. Again, when he was offering sacrifice, the soothsayer Spurinna warned him to beware of danger, which would come not later than the Ides of March; and on the day before the Ides of that month a little bird called the king-bird flew into the Hall of Pompey with a sprig of laurel, pursued by others of various kinds from the grove hard by, which tore it to pieces in the hall. In fact the very night before his murder he dreamt now that he was flying above the clouds, and now that he was clasping the hand of Jupiter; and his wife Calpurnia thought that the pediment of their house fell, and that her husband was stabbed in her arms; and on a sudden the door of the room flew open of its own accord.[12]

Suetonius wrote a little more than a century after Julius Caesar's death. Dio Cassius (ca. 155–ca. 235 CE), another Roman historian writing even later, also tells the story of Caesar's assassination, along with omens that foretold the dire event.

As for him, he was warned of the plot in advance by soothsayers, and was warned also by dreams. For the night before he was slain his wife dreamed that their house had fallen in ruins and that her husband had been wounded by some men and had taken refuge in her bosom; and Caesar dreamed he was raised aloft upon the clouds and grasped the hand of Jupiter. Moreover, omens not a few and not without significance came to him: the arms of Mars, at that time deposited in his house, according to ancient custom, by virtue of his position as high priest, made a great noise at night, and the doors of the chamber where he slept opened of their own accord. Moreover, the sacrifices which he offered because of these occurrences were not at all favorable, and the birds he used in divination forbade him to leave the house. Indeed, to some the incident of his golden chair seemed ominous, at least after his murder; for the attendant, when Caesar delayed his coming, had carried it out of the senate, thinking that there now would be no need of it.[13]

So according to Suetonius some of the omens were the disturbance of bones, which heralded the death of a son of Ilium slain at the hands of his countrymen, horses that refused to graze, the words of a soothsayer, the flight of a bird, and a door opening on its own. According to Dio Cassius, some of the omens were noises made by a statue and a door opening on its own. As we have seen earlier, signs are seen by the eye of the beholder.

Suetonius also tells the story of another sign having to do with Caesar, but not in reference to his assassination:

As the Deified Julius was cutting down a wood at Munda and preparing a place for his camp, coming across a palm tree, he caused it to be spared as an omen of victory. From this a shoot at once sprang forth and in a few days grew so great that it not only equaled the parent tree, but even overshadowed it; moreover many doves built their nests there, although that kind of bird especially avoids hard and rough foliage. Indeed, it was that omen in particular, they say, that led Caesar to wish that none other than his sister's grandson should be his successor.[14]

Of course, not everyone in the ancient world believed in omens. Several thinkers challenged the idea. Cicero has one of the most sustained critiques against the notion of omens, signs, or divination, questioning and ultimately dismissing the idea that human beings can predict future events from present signs. He uses derisive terms such as *laughable* and *absurd*, and in referring to examples of divination, he claims they are "not pertinent at all." Regarding an example of cocks crowing, Cicero says it would have really been something if a fish had crowed. But cocks crow all the time, so how or why would the gods choose to communicate to human beings by a crowing cock? Instead, he encourages his dialogue partner to explore the reason for the purported sign, and undoubtedly it will be found to be due to nature.

In addition to Cicero, Diogenes Laertius (*Lives* 7.149), Minucius Felix (Oct. 26.16), and perhaps not surprisingly the Christian theologian (though later declared a heretic) Origen (*Contra Celsum* 8.45) all argue against omens. But the dismissive tone of a philosopher or natural scientist is often no match for frightened human beings struggling to ascertain meaning from everyday events, signs, or omens.

In the Second Punic war (218–201 BCE), when the feared Carthaginian general Hannibal was marching down the boot of Italy with Rome in his sights, the Romans sent their own general Flaminius with his legions to face the enemy. Flaminius camped at Arretium (modern-day Arezzo in eastern Tuscany) where he came close to the Carthaginian army. We pick up the story from Cicero's *De Divinatione*. In the story the protagonist Quintus claims that Flaminius discounted the signs and omens that were given to him and instead led the army to defeat.

> Again, did not Gaius Flaminius by his neglect of premonitory signs in his second consulship in the Second Punic War cause great disaster to the State? For, after a review of the army, he had moved his camp and was marching towards Arretium to meet Hannibal, when his horse, for no apparent reason,

suddenly fell with him just in front of the statue of Jupiter Stator. Although the soothsayers considered this a divine warning not to join battle, he did not so regard it. Again, after the auspices by means of the tripudium had been taken, the keeper of the sacred chickens advised the postponement of battle. Flaminius then asked, "Suppose the chickens should never eat, what would you advise in that case?" "You should remain in camp," was the reply. "Fine auspices indeed!" said Flaminius, "for they counsel action when chickens' crops are empty and inaction when chickens' crops are filled." So he ordered the standards to be plucked up and the army to follow him. Then, when the standard-bearer of the first company could not loosen his standard, several soldiers came to his assistance, but to no purpose. This fact was reported to Flaminius, and he, with his accustomed obstinacy, ignored it. The consequence was that within three hours his army was cut to pieces and he himself was slain. Coelius has added the further notable fact that, at the very time this disastrous battle was going on, earthquakes of such violence occurred in Liguria, in Gaul, on several islands, and in every part of Italy, that a large number of towns were destroyed, landslips took place in many regions, the earth sank, rivers flowed upstream, and the sea invaded their channels.[15]

Not only was the Roman army defeated at the Battle of Lake Trasimeno (about twenty miles south of Arretium) but Flaminius himself was killed. Flaminius was blamed, among other things, for discounting the ominous portents.

Yet, in the same work by Cicero, *De Divinatione*, he himself speaking as the antagonist in book 2, critiques the Stoic notion of fate, the idea that all is governed by predeterminism. He likewise critiques portents and divination in saying,

> Again, if it was the will of Fate that the Roman army should perish at Lake Trasimenus in the Second Punic War, could that result have been avoided if the consul Flaminius had obeyed the signs and the auspices which forbade his joining battle? Assuredly not. Therefore, either the army did not perish by the will of Fate, or, if it did (and you are certainly bound as a Stoic to say that it did), the same result would have happened even if the auspices had been obeyed; for the decrees of Fate are unchangeable. Then what becomes of that vaunted divination of you Stoics? For if all things happen by Fate, it does us no good to be warned to be on our guard, since that which is to happen, will happen regardless of what we do. But if that which is to be can be turned aside, there is no such thing as Fate; so, too, there is no such thing as divination—since divination deals with things that are going to happen. But nothing is "certain to happen" which there is some means of dealing with so as to prevent its happening.[16]

Great thinkers have pondered these questions for centuries, even millennia. These questions attract us too. The idea that all things might be governed by fate, or perhaps preceded by omens or signs is powerfully engaging.

Berghoff Omen

Omens are not relegated to ancient history alone. Haus der Deutschen Kunst was a Nazi-era modern art museum in Munich, designed by architect Professor Paul Ludwig Troost, and built with public funds. Adolf Hitler laid the cornerstone himself. After a speech wherein Hitler proclaimed Munich the "capital city of German art," he struck the cornerstone with a silver hammer so strongly that the hammer broke. There was a superstition that if the hammer broke the architect would die. Goebbels quickly said, "When the Fuhrer strikes he strikes mightily," but that did not reassure the crowds or even Hitler. Thus Hitler, the crowd, and Troost himself considered it a bad omen. A few days later Troost was hospitalized for angina pectoris and died a few months later of pneumonia.[17] Such an occurrence surely convinced many that the omen of the broken hammer had been fulfilled.

About eighteen months later Hitler launched his invasion of Poland. As preparations were being made for that fateful attack, the northern lights were visible from Hitler's Berghoff. Albert Speer, a close ally who was also minister of armaments and war production, was there that evening and wrote,

> In the course of the night we stood on the terrace of the Berghoff with Hitler and marveled at a rare natural spectacle. Northern lights of unusual intensity threw red light on the legend-haunted Untersberg across the valley, while the sky above shimmered in all the colors of the rainbow. The last act of the Gotterdammerung could not have been more effectively staged. The same red light bathed our faces and our hands. The display produced a curiously pensive mood among us. Abruptly turning to one of his military adjutants, Hitler said: "Looks like a great deal of blood. This time we won't bring it off without violence."[18]

When Hitler said, "This time," he was contrasting the planned invasion of Poland with the relatively easy annexation of Austria and Czechoslovakia. And indeed, the invasion of Poland on September 1, 1939, has become a marker for the start of World War II. Two days later the UK and France declared war on Germany. But for our purposes we recognize that omens are not limited to the ancient world; the Berghoff Omen prominently testifies to that. And like so many signs and portents, they mean something to the one who makes them meaningful.

Entrails

As we saw from the example of General Flaminius in the Second Punic War, one of the ways ancient Romans discerned omens and signs was by examining the entrails of sacrificed animals, often chickens or other birds. Suetonius tells us of a particularly favorable omen concerning Augustus in his first consulship. When he was taking the auspices (the term means literally, "looking at the birds") twelve vultures appeared to him as to Romulus. When Augustus slaughtered the sacrifice, "the livers within all of them were found to be doubled inward at the lower end, which all those who were skilled in such matters unanimously declared to be an omen of a great and happy future."[19]

In a more famous story of discernment by entrails, during the First Punic War (264–241 BCE), the Roman commander of the fleet, Publius Claudius Pulcher, was ready to attack the Carthaginians. Before he did so, the sacred chickens were brought out, but they would not eat. Publius, eager to attack and to press his advantage quickly grew frustrated with the birds and threw them into the sea crying, "If they won't eat, let them drink!" A disastrous battle followed, which was understood by most to be due to Publius's ire and his sacrilegious behavior. Whether his tossing the sacred chickens into the sea frightened his superstitious or perhaps scrupulous men so much that they lost their thirst for battle is known only to the gods. But the story became prominent and echoed down through the ages.[20]

DREAMS, VISIONS, AND PREMONITIONS

Today there are hundreds if not thousands of books having to do with dream interpretation. From those who see dreams as a window into the psyche, to others who maintain dreams can provide a glimpse into the future, the activity of the brain in its sleeping state is ripe for those who want to find a hidden meaning, pattern, or structure to their lives.

Certainly, from antiquity the interpretation of dreams has provided rich fodder, and a few examples will illustrate this. Julius Caesar, who adopted Octavian (63 BCE–14 CE) as his heir, was assassinated in the senate on the Ides of March (March 15), 44 BCE. As we saw above, the night before he was assassinated, Caesar's wife had nightmares,[21] and Caesar himself dreamt "that he was flying above the clouds, and now that he was clasping the hand of Jupiter."[22] These dreams were understood to have foretold Julius Caesar's impending death.

Caesar's adopted heir, Octavian, son of Atia and Octavius, would eventually ascend to the imperial throne and come to be known as Caesar "Augustus," which means "revered." The Roman historian Suetonius tells us Octavius dreamed that the sun rose from Atia's womb. There was a rumor that Atia had been impregnated by Apollo, the sun god, which would mean Atia's son was "divine." Octavius's dream confirmed the divinity of his son. Atia herself, before giving birth to Octavian, dreamed that her vitals were borne up to the stars and spread over the whole extent of land and sea, which confirmed for her that she had been impregnated by Apollo.[23] Octavius also dreamed that his son "appeared to him in a guise more majestic than that of mortal man, with the thunderbolt, scepter, and insignia of Jupiter Optimus Maximus, wearing a crown begirt with rays and mounted upon a laurel-wreathed chariot drawn by twelve horses of surpassing whiteness."[24] The boy Octavian had quite a reputation to live up to; his promising future had been foretold in dreams, and he was the spawn of Apollo! The skeptic might claim that the dreams only served to further the narrative of Octavian's imperial ambitions. But others saw the dreams confirming reality.

Like the bad dreams that Julius Caesar's wife had before he was assassinated, we read in the Gospel of Matthew that Pontius Pilate's wife was disturbed by dreams the night before Jesus was crucified. "While he [Pilate] was sitting on the judgment seat, his wife sent word to him, 'Have nothing to do with that innocent man, for today I have suffered a great deal because of a dream about him'" (Matt 27:19). Pilate's wife is never mentioned in any other New Testament text. This appears to be a Matthean addition to the story he inherited from the Gospel of Mark, meant to dramatically increase the narrative tension as Pilate is still seated on the (judging) bench prior to ultimately deciding Jesus's fate. Was Matthew the evangelist aware of the story of Julius Caesar's wife? Or did he merely write the account as a good storyteller? Scholars differ. But the notion that dreams communicated future events was fairly commonplace in antiquity.

Matthew the Gospel writer is a fan of dreams. In the opening chapters of the Gospel, Joseph, the "foster" father of Jesus, is advised in a dream to take the unwed but pregnant Mary into his house at Bethlehem, when his prior inclination was to end the betrothment (Matt 1:20–21). Matthew also tells his audience that the Magi were warned in a dream not to return to their home country by the same way, due to Herod's maleficent motives (Matt 2:12). And Matthew also has Joseph learn in a dream that it is safe to return from Egypt (Matt 2:19–20). But because Joseph had again been warned in a dream, he settled his family in Nazareth rather than Bethlehem (Matt 2:22). So, dreams seem to be a favored Matthean narrative device, not only with Pilate and his wife, but in the infancy narrative of Jesus as well.

Perhaps Matthew was inspired by the dreams of another Joseph, the one from the Torah. The Joseph of Genesis was a dreamer too, and by his dreams he saved his family, his own people, and even the people of Egypt (Gen 37:1–11).

Throughout much of the Bible, God communicates with human beings through dreams and visions, which are not always clearly distinguished. For example, Matthew is the only New Testament author to use the Greek term for "dream," *onar*, whereas Luke-Acts uses the words for "vision," (*horama*, *optasia*, and *horasis*). In the New Testament, the revelatory nature of dreams and visions is more important than the dreams and visions themselves.[25]

Due primarily to the prominent Swiss psychiatrist Carl Jung (1875–1961), many modern people may no longer consider dreams to be portends of the future but instead an insight into the human psyche. By this approach, one's dreams often represent symbols or archetypes and can be interpreted to reveal something about the dreamer. In this way, dreams continue to serve as a rich vehicle for meaning in the lives of individual human beings, even if they are not considered a means to the divine. To be sure, there are many who continue to interpret dreams as a window to the future, or the foretelling of coming events.

Closely related to the concept of dreams are premonitions or presentiments, often defined as a feeling or sense that something is about to happen. This too is in the mind of the beholder. One example comes from Hitler, who hated snow. After the Russian winter of 1941–42, when nearly two hundred thousand German soldiers were killed and another seven hundred thousand were wounded, Hitler interpreted his hatred of snow as a "presentiment."[26] He had always hated snow, but it was only after the disastrous results of the Russian invasion with his troops getting bogged down in the winter did Hitler make a connection between them. Was his hatred of snow truly a presentiment of the disastrous invasion? Or was the connection merely in the mind of the beholder?

More recently, in early January 2020, Sheyda Shadkhoo was on a flight from Iran back to Canada. She had been visiting her mother and sisters. Concerned about her safety, she called her husband, Hassan, prior to takeoff. With recent tensions in the region, she wanted reassurance that all would be ok before she had to shut down her phone. About twenty minutes later she and all passengers aboard were dead when the Ukrainian International Airline flight was inadvertently shot down. Hassan says that his wife had a premonition.[27]

An impending sense of doom or fear that something bad is about to happen is attributed to premonition. But how many times do people have that sense followed by nothing particularly bad happening? In these cases, the feeling is dismissed and scarcely given a second thought. In a classic example of "confirmation bias," it is only when the feeling is followed by tragedy that the connection seems clear.

On April 3, 1968, Dr. Martin Luther King Jr. gave a speech known as "I See the Promised Land" but also known as "I've Been to the Mountaintop" or "The Mountaintop Speech," at the Bishop Charles Mason Temple in Memphis, Tennessee. As he was concluding, he talked about the challenges he faced and the trepidation around him. For example, the plane that flew him from Atlanta to Memphis that very morning was delayed due to his being a passenger. The plane was guarded the night before and extra precautions were taken to prevent any tragedy. And then Dr. King concluded his speech with these words:

And then I got into Memphis. And some began to say the threats, or talk about the threats that were out. What would happen to me from some of our sick white brothers?

Well, I don't know what will happen now. We've got some difficult days ahead. But it doesn't matter with me now. Because I've been to the mountaintop. And I don't mind. Like anybody, I would like to live a long life. Longevity has its place. But I'm not concerned about that now. I just want to do God's will. And He's allowed me to go up to the mountain. And I've looked over. And I've seen the promised land. I may not get there with you. But I want you to know tonight, that we, as a people, will get to the promised land. And I'm happy, tonight. I'm not worried about anything. I'm not fearing any man. Mine eyes have seen the glory of the coming of the Lord.[28]

The following day, April 4, Dr. King was assassinated. The conclusion of his speech the night before seemed prophetic, perhaps a premonition. And yet, King had faced violence throughout much of the 1960s, and even earlier. In the same speech on April 3, he referenced the time in 1958 when a deranged person stabbed him in the chest, the blade only millimeters from his aorta. As the doctors told him at the time, he was a "sneeze away from death." If he had died by the blade of the deranged person in 1958, he would never have delivered his "I Have a Dream" speech, not to mention his many other accomplishments in the ten years since.

But as for the "Mountaintop Speech," its poignancy is due largely to its being his last, and to its conclusion where he says he may not make it to the promised land with them. Dr. King knew that the threats were increasing and the situation was becoming more dire. In hindsight, after his death, the speech takes on even more gravitas.

Dreams, visions, and premonitions are often in the eye of the beholder, and only confirmed after the fact. When tragedy strikes, we might look for signs that could have pointed to the calamity. Or, we read certain facts in a new light, and they then take on greater meaning and more significant import. Ultimately, we are the ones discerning meaning from events, sifting through past events to find pebbles of significance.

Chapter Five

NATURAL WONDERS

Men think epilepsy divine, merely because they don't understand it. But if they called everything divine which they do not understand, there would be no end of divine things.

—Hippocrates

In addition to internal or interior experiences like dreams or premonitions, natural wonders and phenomena are ripe for meaning. For most of human history we had little to no idea what was truly up in the sky. Human beings recognized the stars but wondered what they could be. Careful observers of the night sky noted that planets were differentiated from stars in that the former "wandered" (the word *planētēs* means "wanderer" in Greek) around the sky whereas the latter held fixed positions. But what really were these distant lights? In Babylon, learned people watched the night sky and made precise recordings of the positions of the planets and stars. They soon correlated these positions with significant events in their history and the field of astrology was born. If something significant happened the last time Venus and Mars were configured in such a way, then we could logically expect another significant event to happen when this reoccurred. The moon, sun, stars, planets, regular eclipses, comets, and more meant that the sky could be a font of knowledge of future events.[1]

In antiquity, the Roman poet Virgil (70–19 BCE) said that a star guided Aeneas to the place where Rome would be founded.[2] Josephus, speaking about the fall of Jerusalem, says a star in the shape of a sword stood over the city and a comet remained for a year (*Wars of the Jews* 6.289).

One of the many signs that were said to have accompanied Julius Caesar's death was a great comet shining in the sky for seven days, which was interpreted as his soul ascending into the heavens. Here is Suetonius's account:

> He died in the fifty-sixth year of his age, and was numbered among the gods, not only by a formal decree, but also in the conviction of the common people. For at the first of the games which his heir Augustus gave in honor of his apotheosis, a comet shone for seven successive days, rising about the eleventh hour [about an hour before sunset], and was believed to be the soul of Caesar, who had been taken to heaven; and this is why a star is set upon the crown of his head in his statue.[3]

So-called signs in the sky were common in antiquity. The Gospel of Matthew speaks of a "star" (*astera*) in the sky marking the birth of Jesus. This star attracted Magi (a class of Zoroastrian priests/astrologers from Persia) who followed it to find the infant Jesus (Matt 2:1–12). The Magi ask, "Where is the child who has been born king of the Jews? For we observed his star at its rising, and have come to pay him homage" (Matt 2:2). Many scripture scholars maintain that Matthew is using a standard convention of the time by using astral events to signify something important. Perhaps Matthew even had the deification of Julius Caesar, or Virgil's *Aeneid*, in mind when he wrote about Jesus. For Matthew, Jesus is much more important than Julius Caesar or the founding of Rome. But other scholars scrutinize the record to see what, if any, historical sign in the sky Matthew might have had in mind.[4]

Pliny dismisses the notion popular at the time that each person has a star that gives light at the child's birth and fades at the person's death (*Natural History* 2.6). He also speaks about the many events in the sky (stars, moons, suns, comets, etc.) that were understood popularly to be related to human events (*Natural History* 2.28–37).

Pliny's naturalistic understanding of the world and readiness to dismiss fanciful notions of heavenly phenomena portending earthly events would have helped in a case with the Emperor Nero, his contemporary, had he been open to the idea. Or to be more precise, Pliny's advice would have helped an otherwise unnamed nobleman. It happened that Nero was spooked by the appearance of a comet, as an astrologer had informed Nero that it portended the death of someone prominent. Not wanting to fall victim to the portent himself, Nero executed a nobleman. By so doing Nero believed that the omen was satisfied, saving himself.[5]

Aside from the ancient Roman world, Islamic tradition holds that a star rose on the night of Mohammed's birth, and that Moses had his own birth star (Mathnawi, 3.900–902). And there is a Chinese tradition that when the semilegendary Lao-Tze (sixth century BCE) was born, a star fell from the sky, whereas a comet rose with his conception.

So the concept of stars or comets marking the births or deaths of significant people seems to be prominent through human history and in various cultures.

ECLIPSES

The natural, regular, predictable phenomena of solar and lunar eclipses have been known since Babylonian times as mentioned above. Great meaning was often inferred from these natural events. Biblical stories of an eclipse include the Gospel of Luke's depiction of the crucifixion of Jesus. Though the Gospel of Mark (which Luke used as a source) says that at Jesus's death, "Darkness came over the whole land until three in the afternoon" (Mark 15:33), Luke clarifies that this is "because of an eclipse of the sun" (*tou hēliou eklipontos*) (Luke 23:45a, NABRE). No other Gospel writer makes that claim. But this apparent explanation comes with its own difficulties, including that it would have been a three-hour solar eclipse! The longest possible solar eclipse is seven minutes and forty seconds, far from three hours. But like so many things in the New Testament, the author is speaking of theology more than history. In other words, Luke, and Mark prior to him, would likely have had in mind the fulfillment of Old Testament scripture passages about the darkening of sun in the last days (Joel 2:28–32; see also Acts 2:17–21). Luke is simply giving a natural explanation to Mark saying that "darkness came over the whole land." And perhaps Luke had in mind the story of an eclipse that was said to have occurred at the death of Julius Caesar. And at least one author (Pliny) claims that the darkening of the sun at Caesar's death lasted nearly a year.[6] Perhaps in Luke's mind, if there had been an eclipse at Julius Caesar's death, then certainly there would have been one at the death of Jesus.

More than four hundred years prior to the death of Jesus was the Peloponnesian War (431–405 BCE) in which Sparta and Athens fought against one another for decades. Each had alliances with various city-states in the Peloponnesus, thus the name of the war. The war itself had two phases separated by a six-year truce. In the second phase of the war, Athens sent a fleet to Sicily meant to interrupt grain supplies being sent from Syracuse to Sparta. This conflict became known as the Battle of Syracuse. After a series of indecisive engagements with reinforcements arriving from each side, Athens was not doing well and was preparing a retreat. But on that very night (August 27, 413 BCE) there was a lunar eclipse. The Athenian commander, Nicias, consulted a soothsayer/astrologer who said that the eclipse was an omen indicating it was not a good time to set sail. Instead, the recommendation was to stay another month. Here is the story from Thucydides (460–400 BCE), an Athenian general who literally wrote the book on the Peloponnesian War:

> All was at last ready, and they were on the point of sailing away, when an eclipse of the moon, which was then at the full, took place. Most of the Athenians, deeply impressed by this occurrence, now urged the generals to wait; and Nicias, who was somewhat over-addicted to divination and practices of that kind, refused from that moment even to take the question of departure into consideration, until they had waited the thrice nine days prescribed by the soothsayers.[7]

This delay would prove costly to the Athenians as it gave the Syracusans the opportunity to block the harbor. Half the Athenian fleet was lost when it was pushed to the shore. In the end, the survivors were taken into slavery, and Nicias was put to death.

One of the more famous (or infamous) episodes of a lunar eclipse has to do with Christopher Columbus (1451–1506). Schoolchildren are taught that in 1492 Columbus sailed the ocean blue. Fewer might recall that he made successive trips to the "New World" after his first. In fact, he made a total of four trips (in the years 1492, 1493, 1498, and 1502). On his last trip he encountered true danger. By the following summer (1503), Columbus and his crew were stranded in what is now called Jamaica, relying on the native peoples for provisions but showing little appreciation. After many months, the natives grew tired of their ungrateful invaders, and stopped helping them. Columbus knew that an eclipse would happen on March 1, 1504, and he said to the natives that the Christian god was upset at the treatment of him and his crew. As a result, the moon would turn bloodred in three days. On the appointed evening the moon did turn red during an eclipse. The natives panicked and implored Columbus to intercede on their behalf to the Christian god. He agreed, and went into his tent for some time, as long as the lunar eclipse lasted. Upon exiting his tent and returning to the natives, Columbus said that the Christian god was appeased. When the natives saw the moon appear as it usually did, their fears were assuaged. Columbus and his crew had no more difficulties with the natives and eventually left Jamaica.[8]

Natural phenomena in the sky hold potential for great meaning. But like so many other examples we have seen, meaning is in the mind of those who seek it. Those who understand the natural world and the way it works can use this knowledge to take advantage of others. Still, when whole groups of people believe a natural phenomenon holds meaning, then even one with knowledge to the contrary might have difficulty convincing them otherwise. For example, would the Athenians have set sail despite a soothsayer who predicted bad omens? One is reminded of Flaminius's dismissal of the portents at Tresmino. Though he placed little faith in the omens, his soldiers certainly believed in them, and might have been "spooked."

ASTROLOGY

In a 2015 poll, Americans were asked what method predicted the future best.[9] Though about one in three said, "None of the above," more than one in five were confident in horoscopes. One in nine believed in fortune cookies, and about the same number believed in psychic readings.

It might seem strange that only a third of the respondents said, "None of the above." Just as many thought fortune cookies or psychic readings were good predictors of the future.

A man and woman met serendipitously. Each thought the other their "soul mate." When asked how they met, the woman replied offhandedly, "It was written in the stars." Though she might not have meant it that way, such an expression has its roots in astrology and the notion that our lives are predetermined, written in the movements of the stars and the heavenly realm. According to a 2018 Pew study, about a quarter of Christians believe in astrology.[10]

As we saw above, the ancient Babylonian world gave rise to astrology, the idea that the position of the stars and planets in the sky somehow influenced events on earth or could be used to predict the future. Even today, most newspapers still carry an "astrology," or perhaps better termed, "horoscope," column. How many people claim to have the attributes of a Gemini or a Leo because of the day on which they were born? These names refer to the constellation of stars prominent in the zodiac during that time of the year. The zodiac itself is a band of sky about 8 degrees north and south of the path of the sun. The names of the constellations come from Greek and Roman mythology: Aries, Taurus, Gemini, Cancer, Leo, Virgo, Libra, Scorpio, Sagittarius, Capricorn, Aquarius, and Pisces. It should be noted that other cultures have different constellations, different ways of connecting the dots of stars in the night sky. It is not surprising that different cultures developed different images from the same "dots."

Today astrologers use the twelve constellations from Greek and Roman mythology to make much of whether a certain planet is rising in a constellation, resulting in some special meaning. As astrologers seem to follow a rigid structure and pattern (the movement of the stars and planets), their work can seem to have a quasi-scientific certainty. But when scientific standards are applied to astrology, then the predictions that human beings make based on the rigid structures and patterns of the stars and planets cannot withstand examination.

The horoscopes published in newspapers, magazines, and on websites, are so generic as to be nearly meaningless. How exactly does the rising of a planet in a certain constellation affect my life on earth? The late popular astronomer Carl Sagan (1934–96) pointed out that the gravitational pull of a doctor delivering a baby has more force on the baby than does the planet Mars, in part because the doctor, though much smaller than the planet, is so much closer.[11]

Even so, astrology and horoscopes continue to be for some a harmless means of entertainment that can provide meaning to daily life. Yet astrology is not harmless, especially for those who take great stock in the meaning of horoscopes. During World War II, Himmler's secret intelligence service employed an astrologer by the name of Karl Ernst Krafft.[12] This same astrologer had predicted the Munich beer hall bombing. Krafft also consulted some "Nostradamus prophecies" and pronounced them fulfilled when Germany took France. He further claimed that the Nostradamus prophecies said London would fall in 1940.[13] For those in leadership positions in Nazi Germany, these horoscopes provided confirmation.[14]

Not to impute any similarity to the Nazis, President Ronald Reagan's calendar was also governed by an astrologer, Joan

Quigley, at the instigation of his wife, Nancy. In her memoir, *My Turn*, Mrs. Reagan speaks of how she consulted the astrologer: "I'm scared every time he leaves the house."[15] Quigley's own account of her time with the Reagans relates just how much astrology guided their decision-making.[16]

There have been countless figures, famous and ordinary, who have consulted astrologers and horoscopes through the centuries. Astrology is another way of making meaning of our experience of the world. In fact, there are nearly ninety-five thousand psychic "businesses" in America, which generated some two billion dollars in revenue in 2018 alone.[17]

Related to astrology and other modes of fortune-telling is "reading tea leaves," known more formally as "tasseography" or "tasseomancy." Here the "wisdom figure" or "fortune-teller" uses not a crystal ball or special cards, but the remnants of tea leaves from a cup (thus, *tasseos,* the Greek word for "cup"). The fortune-teller discerns a pattern in the leaves and the way they cling to the cup after the tea has been consumed. The invention of teabags has mostly done away with tea leaf remnants.

Reading one's fortune or future is not limited to tea leaves. Reading palms and discerning (or creating) meaning from the lines on one's palms can be harmless fun, as can reading fortune cookies. In an early episode of *The Simpsons*, Homer is on a date with a woman who is not his wife. An extramarital affair is in the air as they dine together at Madame Chao's, a local Chinese restaurant. After dinner, Homer's fortune cookie reads, "You will find happiness with a new love," and he responds, "What's the point. I can't fight fate." The scene then moves to the kitchen where the staff realizes they have run out of "You will find happiness with a new love" cookies, so they open a barrel of "Stay with your wife" cookies.[18]

LIGHTNING

Aside from tea leaves, palm readings, fortune cookies, or horoscopes that use the stars and objects in the night sky, to which many turn to find meaning, a myriad of other natural phenomena in the sky are thought to do the same. One is a random lightning strike. With over forty lightning flashes per second across the globe, there are more than one billion flashes per year. In the contiguous United States alone, "an average of 20,000,000 cloud-to-ground flashes have been detected every year since the lightning detection network (NLDN) covered all of the continental US in 1989." In fact, the chances of a human being struck by lightning in a lifetime of eighty years is about 1 in 15,300.[19] It is no surprise that with so many lightning strikes, some of these strikes seem to have auspicious timing.

There are so many stories, historical and modern, of lightning strikes happening at ominous times that only a few examples here will illustrate the point.[20] Suetonius says that in the ancient town of Velitrae (birthplace of Caesar Augustus, modern Velletri), part of its wall had been struck by lightning centuries before the Common Era, while Rome was still emerging as a powerful city-state. The people of Velitrae interpreted the lighting strike to mean that a citizen of theirs would one day rule the world. They maintained belief in this interpretation to such a degree that they made war on Rome many times to their own near annihilation, especially in the fourth century BCE. Only after Octavian, or Caesar Augustus, came to the throne in the waning years of the first century BCE did the meaning of the sign become clear: Caesar Augustus, a citizen of Velitrae, had become ruler of the world.[21] If only the warmongering citizens of fourth-century BCE Velitrae had known that it would take several centuries for the sign to be fulfilled!

In more recent times, lightning and a clap of thunder occurred when England declared a war with Germany, marking their entry into the Second World War.[22] After the war, the United States experienced a British invasion of its own with the advent of four Liverpudlian rockers known as the Beatles. They became so influential that, for some, their prominence rivaled that of religion. On March 4, 1966, an article from the *London Evening Standard* featured a profile of John Lennon in which he was quoted as saying that the Beatles were more popular than Jesus.[23] The remark did not make much news in England, but controversy arose in the United States, especially in the South. Radio station KLUE in Longview, Texas, organized a "Beatles Burning," to which teenagers and other youngsters would bring their Beatles records and other paraphernalia. The burning took place on Saturday night, August 13, 1966. In the early hours of the next morning, the station's tower was hit by lightning, knocking the news director, Phil Ransom, unconscious.[24] Individuals were left to discern meaning from the event. Was God unhappy with the Beatles burning and with the news director personally? Did God like Beatles music? Was it simply a fluke?

Another, more recent ominous lightning strike stirred doubts in the minds of some believers. On February 11, 2013, Pope Benedict XVI shocked the world when he announced that he would step down from the papacy, something that had not been done in many centuries. Hours later, lightning struck St. Peter's, sending a shock of a different sort.[25]

The mere fact of a lightning strike with ominous timing can cause human beings to wonder. Is this a literal sign from the heavens? What meaning, if any, are we to make of it? Yet with over one billion strikes per year across the globe, at least one or two might have auspicious timing.

EARTHQUAKES

Human beings will look to signs not only from the heavens and skies but from Earth itself. In the ancient world there were various ideas about the foundations of the Earth, which was not thought to be a sphere. Some thought Earth rested on a turtle, others that it rested on foundational pillars. The following diagram demonstrates the understanding of the Earth that much of the ancient biblical world would have entertained.

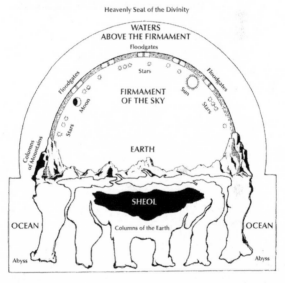

Thus, for many in the biblical world, an earthquake meant that the foundations of the world itself were being shaken. Some biblical books, the Gospel of Matthew in particular, used the narrative of "earthquake" to tremendous effect. For example, Matthew is the only evangelist to say that the crucifixion of Jesus was accompanied by an earthquake. Not only that, this earthquake, the shaking of the very foundation of the

77

world, opened the graves of the dead so that some rose and began walking around!

> Then Jesus cried again with a loud voice and breathed his last. At that moment the curtain of the temple was torn in two, from top to bottom. The earth shook, and the rocks were split. The tombs also were opened, and many bodies of the saints who had fallen asleep were raised. After his resurrection they came out of the tombs and entered the holy city and appeared to many. Now when the centurion and those with him, who were keeping watch over Jesus, saw the earthquake and what took place, they were terrified and said, "Truly this man was God's Son!" (Matt 27:50–54)

Matthew continues with the theme of earthquakes at the resurrection of Jesus.

> After the sabbath, as the first day of the week was dawning, Mary Magdalene and the other Mary went to see the tomb. And suddenly there was a great earthquake; for an angel of the Lord, descending from heaven, came and rolled back the stone and sat on it. His appearance was like lightning, and his clothing white as snow. For fear of him the guards shook and became like dead men. But the angel said to the women, "Do not be afraid; I know that you are looking for Jesus who was crucified. He is not here; for he has been raised, as he said. Come, see the place where he lay." (Matt 28:1–6)

For Matthew, the narrative device of the earthquake recalls the psalms (Pss 68:8; 77:18) that speak of the coming of

God in the image of an earthquake. Further, Jesus himself says that earthquakes, wars, and rumors of wars, will accompany the "birth pangs" signifying the end of the age (Matt 24:6–8).

About a decade or so before Matthew was written, Rome was engulfed in a civil war that coincided with the Roman destruction of Jerusalem. This was sparked by the suicide of Nero and the year of the four emperors in 69 CE from which Vespasian emerged triumphant. Even though Rome was at war with itself, there was still enough imperial will to finish conquering the Jewish holy city and raze it to the ground, courtesy of Titus, son of Vespasian. Could this be what Matthew had in mind by "wars" and "rumors of wars" that would accompany the end times? In addition, about the time the Gospel of Matthew was written, there was a cataclysmic event on the Italian peninsula: the eruption of Mount Vesuvius (August 24, 79 CE) and ensuing destruction of Pompeii and Herculaneum.

Pliny the Younger (61–113 CE) was an eyewitness to the volcanic eruption and the earthquakes that followed. His own uncle, Pliny the Elder, the same naturalist we met earlier, sailed to the site, initially to study what was happening and to rescue a friend and his family. Tragically, he perished along with many others. Pliny the Younger writes gripping accounts of the event in two different letters, which could be the first written accounts of a volcanic eruption.[26] Importantly, he recognized the eruption as a natural event and did not ascribe it to gods, a deity, or any other supernatural cause. His vivid description of Vesuvius has led to similar events being called Plinian eruptions, named after him.

> About one in the afternoon, my mother pointed out a cloud with an odd size and appearance that had just formed. From that distance it was not clear from which mountain the cloud was rising, although it was found afterwards to be Vesuvius. The cloud

could best be described as more like an umbrella pine than any other tree, because it rose high up in a kind of trunk and then divided into branches.[27]

Not everyone in antiquity who witnessed a volcanic eruption could describe it or understand it in naturalist terms. In fact, the very word *volcano* comes from Vulcan, the Roman god of fire, who was associated with the earliest days of Rome. One of the oldest shrines in Rome, near the base of the Capitoline Hill, was dedicated to him.

Today, we do not interpret earthquakes as the shaking of the world's foundations. And we do not understand erupting volcanoes to be caused by Vulcan, or that they are terrible portents sent by the gods.[28] Instead, we have come to recognize that plate tectonics are at work. As the plates shift and collide with each other, stress points are created that result in earthquakes. The molten rock known as magma that spews forth from a volcano comes from deep recesses of the earth.

Though we now have a scientific understanding of earthquakes and volcanoes, some still fall back on ascribing divine intent to these natural actions. Today, even religious leaders attempt to clarify these misinterpretations. For example, in the summer of 2016, Italy experienced a series of earthquakes (regular occurrences in Italy, as they have been for centuries), and unfortunately, several hundred people died. Earlier that same year Italy had approved same-sex civil unions. It did not take much imagination for a radio host on a Catholic station to say that the earthquakes were punishments from God for human sins, namely, the country approving these same-sex unions. The Vatican itself stepped in to condemn that understanding.[29]

Other natural events are taken as omens, though their precise meaning is unclear. For example, Sara Delano Roosevelt, the mother of Franklin Delano Roosevelt, the thirty-fifth President of the United States, passed away on September 7, 1941, at Springwood in Hyde Park, the birthplace and home of FDR. "Minutes after her death, the largest oak tree at Hyde Park toppled to the ground. It was a clear windless day."[30] What would the toppling of the largest oak tree at Hyde Park mean? That is left to the mind of the beholder.

Chapter Six

SUPERSTITION

Many unexplained natural phenomena or their timing can lead one into superstition. The classic definition of *superstition* is "a belief or practice resulting from ignorance," or "not knowing." It can also refer to the "fear of the unknown, trust in magic or chance, or a false conception of causation."[1] Superstitious beliefs and actions might include carrying or wearing a lucky charm, coin, crystal, amulet, or other object, fearing black cats, not walking under a ladder, tossing salt over one's shoulder, knocking on wood, crossing one's fingers, or not opening an umbrella indoors.[2] There is no end to superstitious beliefs, most of which are grounded in ignorance of actual causation of events. But even when actual causation is known, superstitious beliefs can remain. It is not surprising that soldiers are known to become superstitious under periods of great stress.

Athletes, performers, fishermen, gamblers, and many others perform certain superstitious rituals before engaging in an event or contest. Some athletes wear a particular article of clothing or put their shoes on a certain way. Performers might walk in a certain pattern before taking the stage. Fishermen might tip their hat before making a cast. And gamblers have all manner of superstitions from blowing on dice to sitting or standing at special locations at the table. If we query people who perform these actions, they might say that they knew the actual causation was not their actions, but they feel better practicing these rituals.

In one popular superstitious ritual not confined to Catholics, those selling a home bury a statue of St. Joseph in the yard to "guarantee" the sale. If the home does not sell, sometimes the homeowner will bury the statue upside down. But how exactly does burying a statue encourage or precipitate the sale of a home? Those who are convinced do not need an explanation. They simply "know" that it works. Superstitious beliefs give some people meaning and provide a way by which to live their lives, especially when actual causation seems unclear or unexplained. Superstitious beliefs seem to correlate, not only with a lack of knowledge, but also a lack of control. When the homeowner has tried everything else, burying a statue, whether right side up or upside down, might not seem that absurd.

According to a recent (2015) poll,[3] Americans were asked how superstitious they were and about one in four said "somewhat" or "very."

54%	Not at all
22%	Not too
20%	Somewhat
4%	Very

Superstition is as old as humanity itself. Ancient authors like Suetonius and Josephus reflected superstitious attitudes. What might seem odd is that in today's world, with access to scientific knowledge and the application of the scientific method, superstition retains a firm grip on so many. One of the better books about the lingering effects of superstitious belief in our age is *The Demon-Haunted World: Science as a Candle in the*

Dark, written by the late Carl Sagan over twenty-five years ago. In it, he addresses everything from Big Foot, crop circles, alien abductions, UFOs, and more, and he ultimately makes the case for scientifically informed, rigorous thinking. If superstition is belief in a false sense of causation, persistent inquiry and questioning can be part of an effective antidote.

THEURGY

A practice closely linked to superstition is theurgy, though it's a term used infrequently. It might be understood as superstition plus a deity. Both theurgy and superstition display a false sense of causation. Theurgy is the practice of performing rituals to prompt a deity to act in a certain way, or not to act at all. Even though the word *theurgy* is not used often, we see it practiced quite often today by those who recite certain prayers, attend particular services on special days, or wear articles of clothing in the hope or even expectation that something desired will happen. In some ways, theurgy is a sibling of superstition.

Though it can be comforting to consider that life events are guided by the gracious hand of benevolent providence, at other times human beings want something particular from the gods, now! Perhaps this is reflected in the rain dances of aboriginal peoples or the Aztec people sacrificing to ensure the sun returns.[4]

Wanting or not wanting rain are desires that span time and place. During the Battle of the Bulge in World War II, General George Patton wanted rain to cease so he could initiate an attack. He ordered a prayer to be composed,[5] and when the weather cleared on Saturday, December 23, Patton found beautiful skies for "tank hunting." He said, "'God damn! That O'Neill sure did some potent praying. Get him up here, I want to pin a medal on him." He received a bronze star the next day.[6]

In the late fourth century of the Common Era, during a spate of earthquakes in Greece, a certain Nestorius in Athens was said to have had a vision. He urged the citizens to pay honor to Achilles, so Athens would be protected from the earthquakes. He erected an image of Achilles under a statue of Athena and performed services regularly. Thus, the people attributed the lack of earthquakes in Athens to Nestorius's actions.[7] There are countless examples of this sort throughout ancient history. As moderns we might look on these examples of ancient peoples and understand their desire to stop earthquakes. But do we think that Nestorius's tending to the statue really was the cause of earthquake cessation for a time? For we who do not share the worldview or culture of the ancient Greeks, it can be easier to dismiss the supposed causality.

In the late sixth century of the Common Era, Rome was beset by a terrible plague that killed many, including Pope Pelagius II. A new pope was named, Gregory, who would eventually become known as Gregory the Great. To counteract the plague, Pope Gregory organized a procession imploring the mercy of God. The medieval book *The Golden Legend* tells the story:

> And because the mortality ceased not, he [Pope Gregory] ordained a procession, in the which he did do bear an image of our Lady, which, as is said, S. Luke the Evangelist made, which was a good painter, he had carved it and painted after the likeness of the glorious Virgin Mary. And anon the mortality ceased, and the air became pure and clear, and about the image was heard a voice of angels that sung this anthem: Regina cæli lætare, etc., and S. Gregory put thereto: Ora pro nobis, deum rogamus, alleluia. At the same time S. Gregory saw an angel upon a castle which made clean a sword all bloody,

and put it into the sheath, and thereby S. Gregory understood that the pestilence of this mortality was passed, and after that it was called the Castle Angel.[8]

The vision of St. Michael the archangel sheathing his sword was said to be over the mausoleum of Hadrian, which from that point onward, including today, became known as Castel San'Angelo (Castle of the Holy Angel). And the episode has been depicted in many famous paintings and art works throughout the city of Rome.[9] Here too, like the case of Nestorius above, we ask ourselves how much causation is related to the cessation of the plague. Was it really the procession that Gregory organized? Or perhaps we find ourselves like those who bury a St. Joseph statue in the yard of a home we hope to sell and respond with, "I'll try anything. It can't hurt."

God's help is sought not only in times of pestilence and plague but also in times of war. In 1571 there was a major naval battle between forces allied with Pope Pius V (these forces were self-designated as "The Holy League") and that of the Ottoman Empire, whose official religion was Islam. The Pope was a Dominican, which was (and still is) an order of preachers named after St. Dominic (1170–1221), who is said to have received the Rosary from Mary herself in a vision. As a Dominican, Pope Pius V retained the white robes commonly worn by members of the order then and today. In fact, he began the custom of the pope wearing white that continues today. Pope Pius V was said to have been praying the Rosary, imploring Mary's intercession for the Battle of Lapanto, which took place on October 7, 1571, when he received interior knowledge (perhaps akin to a presentiment?) that the victory was won. Whether the legend has any credibility, the forces of the Holy League did in fact defeat the Ottomans, and the Pope attributed the victory to Mary, calling her Our Lady of Victory. Today, October 7 is still celebrated on the Catholic calendar throughout the world as the memorial of Our Lady of the Rosary. This was not the first or last time a battle victory was attributed to Mary, mother of Jesus. In Rome there is a seventeenth-century baroque church by the name Santa Maria della Vittoria (Saint Mary of the Victory), which commemorates a battle that determined whether Prague would be Catholic or Protestant. As a Catholic church was built to commemorate the victory, it is obvious that Catholic forces won the battle.

Other Christians throughout history and even today will look to God or an intermediary to save them from natural catastrophe. Each hurricane season in Louisiana, for example, many Catholics pray to Our Lady of Prompt Succor (Quick Help). This name comes from an early nineteenth-century story of a nun who wanted a favor. She implored the Virgin Mary, "If you obtain for me a prompt and favorable answer to this letter, I make the promise to have you honored in New Orleans under the title of Our Lady of Prompt Succor."[10] Ever since, miraculous or otherwise unexplained occurrences of shifting winds during hurricanes and other such natural occurrences are attributed to her intercession. Attribution to the Virgin Mary under a vast panoply of titles and names for protection is known the world over.[11]

Aside from a deep Catholic culture that attributes miraculous events to the intercession of Mary, many others are content to thank "God." For example, not long ago an American missionary named John Chau made it his goal to visit a remote island off India and to tell the native peoples there about his faith and evangelize them. On his way he wrote a diary in which he says, "The Milky Way was above and God Himself was shielding us from the Coast Guard and Navy patrols." Yet, his encounter ended in disaster as he was killed by those he had hoped to convert.[12] When human actions closely coincide with otherwise unexplained action, we can ascribe causation, a dangerous conclusion, whether superstitious or theurgical.

Chapter Seven

EVERYTHING HAPPENS FOR A REASON

I see a role in other areas, I don't know what it is yet but I'm not done. This happened for a reason.

—Jerry Falwell Jr. upon resigning from his role as president of Liberty University due to personal indiscretions that violated the conduct policies of the university

I'd like to think it's because God wanted to hear me tell these jokes.

—Stephen Colbert[1]

Many of the sayings or thought categories discussed previously have to do with a theological or providential view of the world. But there are many other sayings that capture an expression of fate, destiny, plan, or serendipity. The saying, "Everything happens for a reason," or its close cousin, "It was meant to be," are widely used in the popular culture by Christians and non-Christians alike. A lengthier quote attributed to everyone from Carrie Bradshaw (character from *Sex in the City*) to the physician and theologian Albert Schweitzer, or simply

"Anonymous," displayed on posters, wall hangings, and cute coffee cups, captures the spirit of the phrase, "Eventually all things fall into place. Until then, laugh at the confusion, live for the moments, and know everything happens for a reason."

Recently a popular memoir, *Everything Happens for a Reason: and Other Lies I've Told Myself*, performed well on the *New York Times* best seller list. The author, Kate Bowler, is a Duke Divinity School assistant professor, a researcher of the prosperity gospel who was living a favored life when she was diagnosed with stage 4 cancer. The memoir is an accounting of sorts of her theological predispositions now that she was faced with the reality of death. When believing that good things happen to good people and bad things have an explanation, how do we interpret stage 4 cancer with a new spouse and a newborn? Rationales and explanations from "This is God's plan," to "God needs another angel," leave the author wanting more.

Classical theologians call the problem of "Why do bad things happen to good people," or "Why do we suffer," theodicy. We recall that much of the Old Testament claims that God rewards those who do his will, and he withholds blessings from those who disobey (e.g., Deut 28). But in the later Wisdom literature of the Old Testament,[2] written centuries after Deuteronomy, the problem of the righteous who suffer is addressed most forthrightly. The Book of Job is perhaps the most prominent and well-known example in that Job, who is perfectly upright in the eyes of God, suffers greatly. The reader knows that this suffering happens, not because Job deserved it, but because an adversary (which is what the Hebrew, *satan*, means) made a bet with God. The adversary essentially said to God, "Job is good and praises you only because he has a good life. If he were ever to face adversity, he would cease praising you." God takes the bet and Job suffers misfortune. Throughout the many chapters that follow, Job's three friends ask why Job has faced such misfortune. Surely, they say, he must have done something to deserve it. Job for his part maintains his innocence.

When I am teaching Job, it is at this point in the class discussion that I ask, "What did Job do wrong?" Often, more than half the class comes up with something. But the point of the story is that Job has done NOTHING wrong. He is perfectly just, upright in the eyes of God. He could be considered sinless. Job is only suffering because the adversary claimed that Job praised God solely because he was blessed. If Job lost everything, the adversary said, he would not be praising God. So God allowed that to happen. Why? To win a bet? Job has done nothing to deserve his suffering. And that is precisely the riddle that the Book of Job seeks to address: theodicy, or why bad things happen to good people. In the end, God proclaims himself God, his ways inscrutable (Job 38—41). And Job acquiesces (Job 42:1–6).

So even in the Old Testament Book of Job, theologians were wrestling with the question, "Does everything happen for a reason?" Is there a causal relationship between good things in this life and our good behavior? On the flip side, is there a causal relationship between bad things in this life and our bad behavior? The Roman historian Livy recalls the early days of Rome when "all things turned out well when we obeyed the gods, and ill when we spurned them."[3]

Today, the phrase "everything happens for a reason" is tossed about casually to explain the most mundane aspects of our lives. I'm driving with my friends, hunting for a parking place at the movie theater. Rather than park the car and walk together, I drop off my friends first near the entrance. Then I see that a nearby parking spot has opened: "Everything happens for a reason."

In Arizona, a retired couple was living comfortably in the Phoenix suburbs. Then they received a sizable inheritance but were unsure of how to invest it. Their financial advisor recommended real estate as solid and secure, especially after the 2008 market crash. "Buy low" is the mantra, after all. They were so happy to find a $1.5 million home for which they could now pay cash. Even better, the six-thousand-square-foot home had an elevator. Having always wanted a home with an elevator, they thought that finding this one was a sure sign from the universe. Now, presented with the inheritance and a place with an elevator, they could sell their comfortable home and move into this more opulent one, which would support and facilitate their remaining retirement years. "Everything happens for a reason," they told themselves.

A young couple, both working for the same company, was transferred from Maine to North Carolina. They were eagerly looking forward to buying their first home, as they were only renting in Maine. After looking at over a dozen homes, they found and agreed on one in their price range, in a good school district. They made a full price offer but were edged out by another buyer who had presented their offer only hours earlier. The real estate agent comforted them with the words, "Everything happens for a reason. Your house is still out there." They eventually had to look in other school districts. After another offer on a second house was rejected, the agent told them, "It wasn't meant to be." Finally, the couple settled on a third home on which to make an offer. This one had a map of Maine in the living room. Clearly this was a sign, as their offer was accepted.

Those, like the real estate agent, who express these sentiments are singing in harmony with others who believe some order or rationality is gently guiding daily life. These maxims might help us through a rough patch, or soothe bruised feelings, but upon closer examination do they ring true? Or do they simply appeal to comfortable, privileged people grateful for more? Does everything happen for a reason? Are certain events, such as owning a particular home meant to be? Are there signs that point us toward one path or another? Perhaps there were many homes in which our young couple might have been happy. They saw the map of Maine in the home as a sign, but the first home was in the school district they preferred. Might they have been happy in the first home in the preferred school district? Surely, they would have found and made friends. Their children would have been happy. If the family had been able to purchase the first home, they might have said, "Everything happens for a reason."

Several years and two children later, the young family could not imagine living anywhere else. This house was ideal. The neighbors they met had become good friends, and the teachers in the school were a good match for their children. As for the wealthy couple who inherited more money so they could purchase their ideal retirement home, was the universe working for their benefit? Each couple likely experienced what psychologists call "choice-supportive bias" or "confirmation bias," which we will explore in more detail below. This is a post-decision reevaluation that tends to see one's decisions in the best possible light. In other words, once we have made a choice, we encounter personal pressures to behave consistently with that choice, and those pressures cause us to respond in ways that justify the earlier decision.

WHAT GOES AROUND COMES AROUND

In the *Seinfeld* episode "The Opposite" (Season 5, Episode 22), Jerry experiences a series of events where he ends "even." He loses a gig for one night, but then receives an offer to perform that same night for the same money. He missed a train, but then catches a bus. Elaine puts the principle to the test by asking him for twenty dollars. He hands it to her, she crumples it up and throws it out the window saying, "Let's see if you get the twenty bucks back." Jerry replies, "You could have thrown a pencil out the window and see if that comes back!" Later in the episode, Jerry puts on a jacket and finds a twenty-dollar bill in the pocket! Jerry becomes a proponent of everything evening out, learning not to sweat the small stuff because everything works out in the end...even.

A recent story in the news illustrates a corollary of this principle. A petty thief stole a bottle of ketchup from a restaurant. Shortly thereafter he was in a car accident and his life took a terrible turn. He attributed his bad luck to his stealing the bottle of ketchup. Hoping to turn things around, he made amends by purchasing two bottles of ketchup and leaving them in a bag at the door of the restaurant, with an explanatory note.[4] So we might ask ourselves, did his stealing the ketchup cause the car accident? Is there some cosmic karma that keeps moral acts in order, distributing good to those who do good, and evil to those who cheat and steal? Perhaps it is better for us to recognize that it was the thief in this story who believed that his actions caused him negative outcomes. He attempted to explain his own circumstances, his own "bad luck," and attributed it to stealing the ketchup. His guilty conscience ascribed meaning and causation to his simple act of theft. The thief attempted to construct meaning from the unfortunate events he was experiencing, and then offered to make amends.

SERENDIPITY

On October 13, 1941, Louis and Belle Simon welcomed baby Paul into the world in Newark, New Jersey. When Paul was still a toddler, the family moved to Queens, a short distance from the heretofore unknown Garfunkel family. Paul Simon and Art Garfunkel met in grade school at PS 164 in 1953 and formed a musical duo that would eventually sell over one hundred million records. What were the odds that these two would have found each other, or even more, that their parents would have moved so close together that the boys would meet in grade school? What if Louis and Belle had moved to a different neighborhood, so that Paul had not gone to PS 164? Might Paul and Art have met anyway? What if Louis and Belle had not moved to Queens at all, but stayed in Newark? The simple reflection causes us to wonder how much happens due to serendipity, which is defined as "the occurrence and development of events by chance in a happy or beneficial way."[5]

In another story about a musical artist, when John Lennon was about five years old, he was living with his Aunt Mimi. His father, Alf, had essentially abandoned John and his mother, Julia. For her part, Julia left John in the care of her sister Mimi. Now, when John was five years old, his father, Alf, came back into his life. Alf took the young John to the coastal city of Blackpool with its amusement parks, piers, ice cream, games, and toys. He planned to take John with him to New Zealand where they would live a life of adventure. Alf was days away from leaving when John's mother, Julia, showed up unannounced. Julia was accompanied by her new boyfriend, and she intended to take young John back to Liverpool. When Alf and Julia found themselves at an impasse as to who would take the boy, they turned the decision over to five-year-old John. At first, while on Alf's lap, John said he would stay with his father. Julia promptly turned around and left. After a few moments, young John ran to catch up with his mother and stayed with her.[6] Aside from the traumatic event itself, what would have happened if Alf had left for New Zealand with John a day or so earlier? What if Julia had not been able to find Alf and John in Blackpool? The four lads from Liverpool would never have been. The world would never have known the Beatles. But as it happened, this episode left a mark on John who later alluded to it in his song, "Mother," with its line "Momma don't go/ Daddy come home."

George Harrison is said to have written "While My Guitar Gently Weeps" first by taking inspiration from words chosen randomly when he opened a book. The words were "gently weeps."[7] A comedic story of conveying the happenstance of choosing words at random from turning pages of a book goes like this: A preacher told his congregation that a good method to pray was to flip open the Bible at random, place one's finger on a passage at random and then read it. One congregant tried this at home and was troubled because the passage chosen at random said, "Throwing down the pieces of silver in the temple, he departed; and he went and hanged himself" (Matt 27:5). Upset with this passage, the fervent believer closed the Bible and tried again, only to randomly choose, "Go and do likewise" (Luke 10:37).

Each human story is daily punctuated with serendipity and by necessity. Only occasionally do we look back to ascertain meaning from these everyday events. Yet, as we saw earlier with *Back to the Future* and *Sliding Doors*, cinema loves serendipity. And it's ever present in times of war. It seems it was only by chance that Churchill was not killed or injured by a bomb during the London blitz in World War II, or that George Washington survived riding through a hail of bullets many times in his military career. Examples are countless throughout history.

As we consider some of the events that seem to have swung on chance or fate, an entire industry based on contrafactual narratives has developed. What if the Greeks had been defeated by the Persians in the fifth century BCE? What if the Roman general Germanicus had not been killed in battle, thus saving Rome from Nero? What if, in 1571, the Ottoman Empire had defeated the navy allied with the pope? Or consider John Laurens from South Carolina, friend of Alexander Hamilton, who fought in the Revolutionary War and was a supporter of freedom for those slaves who fought against the British. Laurens was killed in battle at the age of twenty-seven. Had he lived, he certainly would have shaped the Continental Congress and the birth of the nation. How would his voice have contributed to the debates about slavery in the early days of the republic? Or what if the United States had repelled the surprise attack on Pearl Harbor in 1941?

We might also ponder lost works of art, writing, and literature. What more would we know of the ancient world if the biography of Agrippina the Younger (15–59 CE) had survived? Few works from women have come down to us from the Roman world, and Agrippina herself was one of the most prominent women of her time, related to four different emperors. She was great granddaughter of Caesar Augustus. Her father was Germanicus (mentioned above) who was heir apparent until he was killed in battle. Her older brother became Emperor Caligula (r. 37–41) who exiled her. Later she became the fourth wife of the emperor Claudius (r. 41–54) before her own son Nero (r. 54–68) became emperor. It's said that the first five years of Nero's reign were the best the empire had seen since the time of Augustus, but primarily because Agrippina herself held the reins of power. Eventually, Nero had his mother killed, and so began the road to his own demise and eventual suicide. But wouldn't we love to know the story from her point of view? Sadly, her autobiography is lost.

For those more accustomed to the Bible than the classical world, we might consider what Paul says in 1 Corinthians 5:9, when he reminds the community, "I wrote to you in my letter not to associate with sexually immoral persons." The perceptive reader might ask herself, I thought this was the *first* letter to the Corinthians; he's referencing an earlier letter? What would we call *that* letter? So perhaps what we know as the First Letter to the Corinthians is really the second, and what we know as the Second Letter to the Corinthians is really the third! We don't have that earlier letter referenced in 1 Corinthians 5:9. It's been lost to history by chance or happenstance. As an aside, academics play a theological parlor game about what would happen if we, without a doubt, "found" this earlier letter. Would it be considered scripture?

Aside from letters and works for which we have only references, consider the finding of the Dead Sea Scrolls in 1948. These documents are the oldest manuscripts of certain biblical books that we have; they also preserve other documents from antiquity. As the story goes, a Bedouin goat herder was throwing rocks into caves around the Dead Sea one day when he heard clay breakage. Going in to explore, he found clay vessels holding scrolls. Eventually several caves were found to hold scrolls, fragments, and clay vessels. Some scrolls were burned as fuel on cold nights, and other scrolls were sold and eventually came into the hands of antiquities dealers, and from there they found their way to scholars. Once scholars determined what these scrolls were, access was severely limited. About a dozen experts pored over these texts for decades in sunlit rooms with the scrolls taped down with cellophane tape. The role of chance, greed, carelessness, selfishness, and pride all played a role in this continuing saga. It's fascinating and tragic to think of the scrolls that survived for two millennia in clay jars only to be burned as fuel on a cold desert night. What knowledge did we lose? What stories or insights would they have told had they been translated?

NUMEROLOGY

Another way people discern meaning and attempt to interpret events in their lives is by numbers. Some of the most famous unlucky numbers in the west are 666 and 13. Many people even have their own "lucky" number.

666

The negative associations with the number 666 come primarily from the Book of Revelation where it is said to be the "sign of the beast." "This calls for wisdom: let anyone with understanding calculate the number of the beast, for it is the number of a person. Its number is six hundred sixty-six" (Rev 13:18). The note in the New American Bible on this verse sums up the matter well.

> Each of the letters of the alphabet in Hebrew as well as in Greek has a numerical value. Many possible combinations of letters will add up to 666, and many candidates have been nominated for this infamous number. The most likely is the emperor Caesar Nero (see note on Rev 13:3), the Greek form of whose name in Hebrew letters gives the required sum. (The Latin form of this name equals 616, which is the reading of a few manuscripts.) Nero personifies the emperors who viciously persecuted the church. It has also been observed that "6" represents imperfection, falling short of the perfect number "7," and is represented here in a triple or superlative form.

The number 666 has come to mean nearly anything associated with evil or the devil himself, portending doom. And the number is applied to all sorts of people, places, and things. For example, Ronald Wilson Reagan (each of his names has six letters) was said by some to be the harbinger of the fulfillment of the prophecies in Revelation. On February 2, 2018, the Dow lost 666 points. But like so many things, in the case of the number 666, meaning is in the eye of the beholder.

13

About as old as the negative associations of 666 is the association of bad luck with the number thirteen. We see this today in many different and even strange ways. The Apollo 13 space mission had innumerable challenges. Was it because of the numeral in its name? Despite the challenges, Apollo 13 did not have an electrical fire on the launchpad that killed all the astronauts as did Apollo 1 (as it came to be known), on January 27, 1967, or explode like the Space Shuttle Challenger on January 28, 1986. The number thirteen itself does not a disaster make.

And yet, as only one example among hundreds, the Hilton Anaheim Hotel in California has no thirteenth floor, but there is a fourteenth. When guests get into the elevator there is no option for thirteen. A discerning guest might ask, does the Hilton Anaheim not have a thirteenth floor? Maybe, but our discerning guest might also recognize that the fourteenth floor is fourteenth in name only. But does merely naming the thirteenth floor "fourteen" really make it so? Apparently, such renaming calms the anxieties of those who fear the number thirteen. And yet, if we count the floors from the outside of the building, we'll count thirteen.

According to the 2015 poll cited earlier,[8] less than half of Americans (45%) thought that there should be a row thirteen on an airplane, just like any other row. Eighteen percent said that row thirteen should always be an exit row and more than one third (37%) said there should not be a row thirteen on an airplane at all.

Aside from these "unlucky" numbers, many people have their own "lucky" numbers that they play with lottery tickets, at the horse races, in a variety of other gambling scenarios, or even in day-to-day life like hunting for parking spaces. But is it the number itself that is lucky or unlucky? Or is it the association we place upon it?

Human beings seek many various means to structure, order, and explain the events in their lives. Believers may use terms such as *God's plan* or *God's will*. Others may ascribe events to the divine but prefer terms such as *providence*. Still others discern a benevolent force or power in the world they refer to as "fate" or "destiny," which may be preceded by certain signs. There are many more who might claim that "everything happens for a reason" or use some other nonreligious or nontheological means of explaining the naturally unfolding events in daily life.

Countless numbers of human beings, likely most of us, seek to find a structure or pattern from the events of daily life, or to provide a means of understanding these same events. In this way, we human beings make meaning for ourselves. It has been said that the most human of all human needs is the desire to find and fulfill a meaning in one's life or situations.[9]

Viktor Frankl notes that God is often portrayed as a being most concerned with how many people believe in a particular creed or god. People are told, "Believe and everything will be okay," but that is doomed to failure. One cannot be commanded to believe just as one cannot be commanded to laugh. Hearing a joke causes laughter. And experience of the divine causes belief.[10]

Let us imagine, as a thought experiment, that we are able to set aside notions of God's plan, God's will, providence, fate, and destiny, and consider that the world functions as it does without such a benevolent or other force guiding events. Would we as human beings be able to make sense or make meaning out of such a way of looking at the world? Would we be able to construct meaning in a world that operates largely by chance within the bounds of the laws of physics, chemistry, biology, and the other hard sciences?

Chapter Eight

MEANING MAKING

The Auschwitz prisoner and psychiatrist Viktor Frankl (1905–97) wrote *Man's Search for Meaning*, which was published in German in 1946. It sold millions of copies and has been rated one of the ten most influential books in the United States.[1] Born in Vienna, Austria, Frankl displayed an early interest in Freud and even impressed the father of psychology with a paper he wrote as a sixteen-year-old boy. By 1930, Frankl had earned his medical degree and was heading a neurology and psychiatry clinic in Vienna.

With the rise of anti-Semitism and Nazism, Frankl was eventually arrested and sent to Auschwitz from 1942 until the liberation of the camp in 1945. During his imprisonment he kept notes that would form the basis of his book, in which he claims,

> Man's search for meaning is the primary motivation of his life and not a "secondary rationalization" of instinctual drives. This meaning is unique and specific in that it must and can be fulfilled by him alone; only then does it achieve a significance which will satisfy his own *will* to meaning.[2]

One primary and perhaps shocking insight he has is that there is no "plan" or "providence," but instead there is meaning making amid chance, or "transitoriness," to use a term from Frankl. It is said that his survival in the concentration camp depended on blind luck;[3] there was no plan for him to survive and publish his work. Frankl's insights are reflected by several other scientists and philosophers, whether they have been influenced by Frankl directly or indirectly, such as Richard Dawkins who says, "The truly adult view, by contrast, is that our life is as meaningful, as full and as wonderful as we choose to make it."[4] Other thinkers such as Dan Siegel note that "being involved in something larger than a personal self creates a sense of meaning and well-being—an essential part of the experience of 'happiness.'"[5]

For one who survived the horrors and atrocities of the Nazi camp at Auschwitz, Frankl's reflections on the meaning of life are particularly profound. He claimed that in discerning the meaning of life, one should not ask what the meaning of one's life is. Rather he insists that one ought to recognize that it is "he" who is asked. In a word, each person is questioned by life and each person can only answer to life by answering for his or her own life. To life, one can "only respond by being responsible."[6] Later, Frankl continues that the transitoriness of our existence in no way makes it meaningless. But it does constitute our responsibleness; for everything hinges upon our realizing the essentially transitory possibilities. We constantly make choices concerning the mass of present potentialities. Which of these will be condemned to nonbeing and which will be actualized? Which choice will be made an actuality once and forever, an immortal "footprint in the sands of time"? At any moment, one must decide, for better or for worse, what will be the monument of his existence.[7]

As we might realize, such an attitude as Frankl's places tremendous responsibility on the individual person. Rather than ascribe events to some plan, or to providence, Frankl recognizes and even embraces the "transitoriness of our existence." It can be challenging to explore and ultimately embrace such transitoriness, or chance, especially concerning our own personal existence. One thought experiment might help.

DIFFERENT PARENTS?

Anyone with children has likely heard one of them say something like, "Just think if I had a different mom or a different dad. How would my life be different? How would it be changed?" But there is no such way that any individual could have had a different biological mother or biological father, for then we would be speaking about a *different* individual. Ultimately, it is a fallacy to think any human being could have been born to different parents, just as it is a fallacy to think that any human being could have been born at a different time or age. Each human being is a product (literally) of biological parents, who themselves were a product of their biological parents, and who were a product of their biological parents as well, going back generations and generations. Each person is bound to a *particular* time and to a *particular* place, with unique DNA, based on a particular mother and a particular father, and the generations before them. Even if a person is raised by a parent or parents whose DNA is not shared, as in a case of adoption, each person, each one of us, could not have been born at any other time or place or to any other parents.

There have been several recent troubling stories about fertility clinic doctors using their sperm rather than that of the selected donor to impregnate women seeking those services.[8] Naturally, identity crises, shock, and revulsion abounded. The cases pose troubling and profound questions, including the moral culpability of the doctors. But finding that one's parents are not who they seemed to be is a challenge made more prominent by modern services such as DNA tests. These tests are opening the door to secrets that had been closed. Those who thought they were related might find that a more complex narrative was at work. One story of children switched at birth illustrates this.

Over a century ago, in a New York hospital, a Jewish boy was mistakenly sent home with an Irish family as Jim Collins, whereas the Irish boy was sent home with the Jewish family as Philip Benson. Jim Collins was so proud of his Irish heritage that "Danny Boy" was sung at his funeral. Neither family apparently suspected a thing, and the mix up did not come to light until a later DNA test showed that a descendant of Jim Collins was part Ashkenazi Jewish. How could she be Jewish, she thought, when she had been born into an Irish family? After a great deal of research over many years, the story came together.[9]

The boys themselves had radically different upbringings. Jim's mother died when he was young. His father, a longshoreman, was unable to cope with multiple children and no wife. He placed the children in an orphanage and died shortly thereafter. Jim was adopted, raised in a troubled home, and never finished high school. Philip was raised in an intact home with many luxuries. Yet neither child was aware they were with the "wrong" family. Further, what of their descendants and their stories? The grandchildren literally owe their existence to an administrative error. Does such knowledge change who we are? Or who we think we are? Such stories might not be as rare now that we have more access to DNA tests. Family secrets or indiscretions may come to light. The human story is complicated, rarely neat and tidy.[10]

HOMUNCULUS

Let's take this thought experiment about the transitoriness of our existence a step further. Each act of sexual intercourse has the potential of producing a new individual human being, whether that act of intercourse happens between married persons, a one-night stand between passing strangers, an act of adultery, an act of sexual violence such as rape, or a myriad of other scenarios. In addition, technology now allows in vitro fertilization and surrogate motherhood without intercourse. There are countless scenarios in which a child might be conceived. And even in the best-planned circumstances, chance is ever present.

Biologically speaking, the role chance plays in the creation of any human being is especially pronounced. The mature male human being produces ejaculate containing roughly 210 million sperm cells. But only one of these nearly one quarter of a billion sperm cells will unite with the egg to produce a unique human being. What a lottery! We might be reminded of Frankl's comment about the mass of present potentialities, yet in this case all but one is condemned to nonbeing.

Even then, when a single sperm cell fertilizes the egg, that fertilized egg must implant in the uterine wall, which does not happen in each case. Once implanted, there is no guarantee that the fertilized egg will develop and grow into an embryo, blastocyst, and eventually a fetus. The chance that any of us is present here reading this book goes back to that encounter when the odds were against us, more than 200 million to 1. And yet, here we are. Such odds and the serendipity of any single human being existing on this earth are reflected in this poem by Aldous Huxley (1894–1963), an English writer best known for *Brave New World* (1932):

> A million million spermatozoa
> All of them alive;
> Out of their cataclysm but one poor Noah
> Dare hope to survive.

And among that billion minus one
Might have chanced to be Shakespeare,
another Newton, a new Donne—
But the One was Me.

Shame to have ousted your betters thus,
Taking ark while the others remained outside!
Better for all of us, froward[11] Homunculus,
If you'd[12] quietly died!

—Aldous Huxley (1920)

Huxley recognized that the odds are against each one of the 210 million, and yet, for a human being to be conceived, one sperm does in fact fertilize the egg, producing a unique DNA sequence. Once that unique human being is born, it seems natural to think that she or he was "meant to be." But in the moment, chance reigned supreme.

Of course, chance applies to species beyond humans as well. The role of chance in the propagation of every species is critical to that species's success. The world is imbued with chance and infused with possibility and unrealized potentiality. Nature shows us how many seeds are produced by a vast number of living things, from plants and insects to animals. How many acorns produced by an oak tree each autumn germinate and become saplings? How many saplings grow to maturity to produce acorns of their own? Consider too the larvae of mosquitoes in a pond, many of which are consumed by predators or otherwise do not reach maturity. The same is true of animals, including humans. Not only is nature imbued with chance, accompanied by unrealized potential every day, but we too as human beings interact with the natural world and the mass of potentialities, condemning some to nonbeing while actualizing others. In so doing we imprint footprints on the sands of time as Frankl would say. Even more, we essentially direct future possibilities and options by our choices today.

CHANCE

The world certainly has order, and it is governed by discernible laws of physics and motion, as Isaac Newton (1642–1727) discerned. Newton's law of universal gravitation explains the motion of an apple falling from the tree as well as Earth's orbit around the sun. This model worked, and continues to work, well. Newtonian physics became known as "classical determinism," represented by the model for the universe of an intricate clock. This machine moved according to its own mechanistic structure, needing nothing extrinsic.

Einstein and others in the twentieth century began to challenge the Newtonian model. Newtonian physics still works of course, but at a more fundamental, submicroscopic level, Newtonian physics no longer applies. This is partly because at a fundamental level there is an intrinsic and essential element of chance or probability. Quantum mechanics expresses this by saying such things as there is a 20 percent chance that this particle will be here and not there. That chance remains until the particle is measured. Only then is it "here" and not "there." So even though it may appear that the universe follows a clockwork pattern, at a minuscule level, it seems chance and probability reign supreme.

Though chance plays a role at the subatomic level, chance or probability also plays a different role in the realm of Newtonian physics. Weather might be one easy way to recognize this. Weather reports often speak of a chance of rain, and the accuracy of weather reports increases inversely related to the time until the weather event. So a weather prediction made three hours prior to an event will be much more certain than one made three days or three weeks ahead. Indeed, a three-week forecast is essentially worthless. Some who subscribe to a classical deterministic view of the world would say that a system like the weather is so complex with so many competing variables, that we are not able to compute with much precision more than a few days in advance. If only we knew more of the variables and had even better computers, we would be able to predict weather systems with more precision. While there is certainly truth to that, probability is part of our lived experience just the same. We simply do not have access to every variable. We live in a world governed by probability within the laws of physics.

In addition to the offspring of many species, the subatomic world of quantum mechanics, and mundane weather, there are many more examples of chance in the world. We might think of gambling with dice and cards. There is such a thing as the "gambler's fallacy," a type of apophenia, which itself is a condition that seeks to find meaning in unrelated events and circumstances. We have likely seen the gambler's fallacy in action, if not experienced it ourselves.

Try this problem at home. If a person flipping a coin of heads or tails sees results of ten "heads" in a row, what are the chances that the coin will land on "heads" again for the eleventh time in a row? While it may seem counterintuitive, the answer is 50 percent. The previous string of ten "heads" in a row doesn't affect the probability of another "heads" at all. The fact that the gambler believes that the string does affect the probability, or that the gamblers faith that the string has a greater chance of breaking, is precisely the fallacy.

CASTING LOTS

"Luck be a lady tonight," sing the gamblers and gangsters from the 1950s musical *Guys and Dolls*. They see luck as a fickle woman, personifying chance itself. But the gangsters and gamblers who throw the dice have deep roots in human history. The Romans understood the fickle nature of dice and ascribed divine action there as well. The goddess Fortuna (fortune, luck) governed games of chance.

The Book of Proverbs says, "The lot is cast into the lap, but the decision is the LORD's alone" (Prov 16:33). This saying reflects the idea that human beings cast the lot, or dice, but what the dice reveal when they are cast is from God. There are several examples in the Old Testament of seeking to know the will of God by casting lots, which were referred to as the Urim and Thummim (e.g., Exod 28:30; Lev 8:8; Num 27:21; Deut 33:8; 1 Sam 14:41; 28:6; Ezra 2:63; Neh 7:65).

This kind of divination is also reflected in the New Testament. The apostles gathered after the crucifixion of Jesus to replace Judas, one of the Twelve, who had committed suicide. Two candidates were put forward, Joseph and Matthias. "Then they prayed and said, 'Lord, you know everyone's heart. Show us which one of these two you have chosen to take the place in this ministry and apostleship from which Judas turned aside to go to his own place.' And they case lots for them, and the lot fell on Matthias; and he was added to the eleven apostles" (Acts 1:24–26). The story tells the reader that God himself chose between Joseph and Matthias when the lot fell upon Matthias. It should be noted that the selection of bishops (said to be the successors of the apostles) does not happen this way. No longer, perhaps, do ecclesiastical officials believe in the Divine Providence of dice when selecting those for office.

Today, perhaps due to a more sophisticated understanding of math, we recognize how probability plays a role in casting dice. Indeed, the mathematical field of probability grew out of interest in gaming and gambling. Christiaan Huygens (a teacher of Leibniz, one of the founders of calculus) wrote the first book on the topic in the seventeenth century.[13] But even though we have a rational understanding of probability theory now, there is something in the human spirit still drawn to connect the divine to chance.

How many times have we heard about pastors and priests playing the lottery, promising God to give the winnings to the parish, church, school, or other charitable cause? Promising a share of the winnings to God is not limited to clergy. Many people make similar vows, and we may believe most are disappointed. Does God not want to solve the monetary problems of the underfunded parish?

Many people can maintain both at least a rudimentary understanding of probability and hold fast to a belief in the divine, perhaps even divine interaction. How many prayers are said in casinos? And yet, they run a profitable business. Math dictates that eventually the house will win, even if an individual gambler believes that luck, or fortune, is on her side.

The mathematician David Hand wrote a book on the mathematics of chance entitled *The Improbability Principle*. In it he claims, "If we believe there's a single intelligence directing the universe, we ascribe events to chance only because we don't know their cause....This shift leads us to the notion of a deterministic universe, which is following the steps of a master plan, as set up by the one God."[14] Many philosophers, logicians, and statisticians are quick to point out that correlation does not mean causation. But when we maneuver through the world witnessing so many events that are correlated in our own thoughts and mind's eye, it can be a challenge not to draw a cause-and-effect relationship. Did blowing on the dice cause me to roll a seven? "At least it won't hurt to blow on the dice each time," we might think to ourselves, not wanting to jinx anything. Dan Siegel, author of *Mindsight*, claims, "We seek causal links in every sort of experience—even making them up when there are none. The drive for continuity and predictability runs head-on into our awareness of transience and uncertainty."[15]

The poetic beauty of coincidence is a powerful motivating factor in ascribing meaning to events. Studies have shown that those who believe in ESP (extrasensory perception) and related phenomena judge coincidences in random sequences to be more meaningful than nonbelievers.[16] Recently, a man who had been playing the lottery with the same numbers for over fifty years won.[17] Probability indicates that by playing the same numbers consistently for so long, his chances of winning increased. But the fact that he did win makes the coincidence even more compelling.

CONFIRMATION BIAS

The human understanding when it has once adopted an opinion...draws all things else to support and agree with it. And though there be a greater number and weight of instances to be found on the other side, yet these it either neglects and despises, or else by some distinction sets asides and rejects....Men, having a delight in such vanities, mark the events where they are fulfilled, but where they fail, though this happen much oftener, neglect and pass them by.[18]

—Francis Bacon

Have you ever tried to present evidence to support your position to someone who holds a contrary view? How many times does evidence, or the presentation of facts, change someone's opinion or point of view? The answer is not often.

Though each of us likely considers him or herself to be open to evidence and capable of freethinking, we are much more likely to read or support material that already agrees with our point of view. This phenomenon is at the heart of the business models of Facebook, Twitter, and many other social media algorithms, not to mention cable TV "news" and opinion shows. Psychologists call this "confirmation bias," which can also be understood as a tendency to believe more strongly in choices once they are made.[19]

Simply being aware of confirmation bias helps us to be more open to other points of view, or to facts that do not correspond to our otherwise solidly held beliefs. Confirmation bias may also help us explain why we tend to settle into our lives and not make major changes regularly. Confirmation bias can shape the attitude of "no regrets," that some people have; they tend not to see past choices as mistakes or something that might have been done differently or better. Instead, each past choice or experience made me, even confirmed me, as the person I am today. Therefore, "no regrets."

Confirmation bias helps us make meaning of our circumstances. It is necessary for us to move forward in life. The mental energy required to reach back into the past and reevaluate decisions with regularity is often too much for us to expend and still function in the "here and now" at a productive level. In fact, ruminating over past major life decisions, even minor ones, can be debilitating or even become a sign of depression. So, there are certainly benefits to confirmation bias, that tendency to think everything has worked out for the best and that we made the best decision considering the available evidence. This allows us to move forward in life without ruminating over the past. But it also can dissuade us from reexamining our closely held beliefs.

IN THE FACE OF DEATH

I would love to believe that when I die I
will live again, that some thinking, feeling,
remembering part of me will continue.
But as much as I want to believe that, and
despite the ancient and worldwide cultural
traditions that assert an afterlife, I know
of nothing to suggest that it is more than
wishful thinking.

—Carl Sagan[20]

As we progress through life, often preoccupied with day-to-day activities, each of us might occasionally contemplate a time when our own personal existence will be no more. Glancing at an old photograph from the late 1800s, one might conjure up thoughts about the transitoriness of life. Who were they? What were their daily lives like? What was important to them at that moment? What thoughts and activities occupied their lives? What about all those people who were never photographed? A visit to a cemetery might cause one to have similar thoughts. Who were these people? Who remembers them? What stories, if any, are told about them? The words from Ecclesiastes 2:16 come to mind: "For there is no enduring remembrance of the wise or of fools, seeing that in the days to come all will have been long forgotten. How can the wise die just like fools?" When we consider our lives from the perspective of later generations, it can help us reprioritize, reframe, or refocus. As the Psalmist says,

The days of our life are seventy years,
  or perhaps eighty, if we are strong;

even then their span is only toil and trouble;
> they are soon gone, and we fly away. (Ps 90:10)

The Book of Sirach puts it this way:

What are human beings, and of what use are they?
> What is good in them, and what is evil?
The number of days in their life is great if they
> reach one hundred years.
> Like a drop of water from the sea and a grain of
> sand,
so are a few years among the days of eternity.
> (Sir 18:8–10)

The questions of the meaning of life are especially profound when we consider our own death. The scriptures recognize how short life is. The fathers of Vatican II also recognize the quest for meaning in the face of death: "It is in regard to death that the human condition is most shrouded in doubt" (*Gaudium et Spes* 18). At occasional intervals, modern media stories and best-selling books wrestle with the concept of death and what happens to the self when one dies.[21] Much research is being done on extending life and erasing the sometimes fuzzy boundary between life and death. So too, research is being done on near-death experiences and the subjective nature of these experiences.[22]

Perhaps the most urgent occasion for "meaning making" is when we face the death of a loved one, especially sudden, unexpected circumstances like that of an accident, severe illness, heart attack, stroke, or other tragedy. In such heartbreaking cases, many people question the existence of God, wonder why this happened at all, whether something could have been done to prevent it, or whether there is any purpose to human life. During the COVID-19 outbreak in Detroit, a certain man lost several friends. He said, "We know we're born and we're going to die. But when you lose eight people you know well to this virus in two weeks? I'm a religious person, so I'm not going to be the one to question God. But you almost want to ask, 'Really, God, why?'"[23]

The Swiss psychologist Elisabeth Kübler-Ross (1926–2004) outlined five stages of grief—denial, anger, bargaining, depression, and acceptance—in her 1969 classic, *On Death and Dying*. Her model remains prominent in popular circles though other psychologists have proposed different (sometimes more, sometimes fewer than five) stages of grief. Even so, these stages are not thought or meant to be linear but can happen at different times with different individuals. The stages themselves represent human grappling with loss and can be applied to a variety of scenarios beyond death and dying to relationships, employment, moving a home, and more. As Kübler-Ross identified, one can come to "acceptance" of a loss, even if that loss cannot be explained or rationalized.

Recently there was a Catholic priest whose mother died. Both the priest and his mother were well-known in the community, and the church was filled for the funeral, at which the priest presided. After the funeral one of the parishioners said to him, "You must feel so confident knowing there's a heaven and that you'll see your mother again." In a moment of profound honesty, the priest replied, "I hope that's true, but I don't know that's the case." And so, the priest illustrated the difference between knowledge and hope. The object of hope is not seen, as the Apostle Paul says (Rom 8:24). Though many Christians and others believe strongly in life after death and might even think they have "knowledge" through faith, any hope of life after death is just that: hope.[24]

We are reminded that most of the Old Testament (and therefore most of Scripture) does not express a belief in life after death.[25] For example: "We must indeed die; we are then like water that is poured out on the ground and cannot be gathered up. Yet, though God does not bring back to life, he does devise means so as not to banish anyone from him" (2 Sam 14:14, NABRE). Instead of a personal life after death, much of the Old Testament envisions that one lives on through their children. Furthermore, it is thought that God rewards the just in this earthly life. Deuteronomy 28 is a classic example of a theology that claims God rewards those who do his will (vv. 1–14) and withholds blessings and imposes curses (vv. 15–68) on those who disobey. But much more than this chapter conveys that theology; it is predominant in much of the Old Testament.[26]

Not until later books, such as the Wisdom literature, is this "reward/punishment" theology questioned, as we saw above. For example, we recall that in Job the author addresses the question of "sinless" Job's suffering. Job has done everything right in his life and he is blessed by God. Then, seemingly out of nowhere and for no reason, disaster strikes. He loses his children, his home, his land, his crops, and more. Even his wife encourages him to curse God for this turn of fortune, but he will have none of it. In the story of Job, we see past theology questioned, that which claims the good are rewarded in this life while the wicked suffer. It's as though lived experience of the author(s) put the standard theology of "reward/punishment" to the test.

Other Old Testament books recognize that not everyone in this life who is rewarded is good, and not everyone who faces catastrophe or tragedy is evil. One of the earliest explanations of this quandary was to place the blame or punishment on someone else, a child or perhaps an ancestor. Numbers 14:18 conveys this "solution":

> The LORD is slow to anger,
> and abounding in steadfast love,
> forgiving iniquity and transgression,
> but by no means clearing the guilty,

visiting the iniquity of the parents
upon the children
to the third and the fourth generation.[27]

So in that case, if one were suffering it could be due to the behavior of ancestor(s). And not surprisingly, there are other passages in Scripture that question the idea of punishment falling to a later generation.[28] Several solutions are postulated but there is not one that carries the day. Instead, these various solutions live together in the Old Testament for theologians and preachers to pick and choose from.

Even so, the idea that someone is at fault when tragedy happens is reflected in the New Testament too. When a tower fell on some otherwise innocent persons, Jesus himself dismissed a theological explanation:

> At that very time there were some present who told him about the Galileans whose blood Pilate had mingled with their sacrifices. He asked them, "Do you think that because these Galileans suffered in this way they were worse sinners than all other Galileans? No, I tell you; but unless you repent, you will all perish as they did. Or those eighteen who were killed when the tower of Siloam fell on them—do you think that they were worse offenders than all the others living in Jerusalem? No, I tell you; but unless you repent, you will all perish just as they did." (Luke 13:1–5)

At least in this story, Jesus rejects the idea that "bad things happen to bad people." Other gospel stories make the same point. Jesus is asked about the person born blind, "Who sinned, this man or his parents, that he was born blind?" Jesus answers, "Neither this man nor his parents sinned" (John 9:2–3). Yet, there are many Christians today who promote the "prosperity gospel," which assumes we are rewarded in this life for good deeds.

The corollary of course is that tragedy too has an explanation, likely rooted in somebody's sin or transgression.[29] But a familiarity with a more wholistic sense of the Bible should inoculate believers against that ideology. As the Wisdom literature of the Old Testament and Jesus himself explains, bad things happen. To ascribe those unfortunate experiences to the fault of the one who suffers is too simplistic and ultimately not true.

The Book of Job is not the only place that questions the standard "rewards for the good" and "punishments for the bad" theology. Much of Wisdom literature does the same, reflecting on what today might be called the quest for human meaning. Wisdom literature shares with the Old Testament the belief that there is no personal life after death. Instead, the most one might expect, much less hope for, is a shadowy existence in a place referred to as "Sheol." Even from there, one cannot even praise God, as the Book of Job says,

> But mortals die, and are laid low;
> > humans expire, and where are they?
> As waters fail from a lake,
> > and a river wastes away and dries up,
> so mortals lie down and do not rise again;
> > until the heavens are no more, they will not
> > > awake
> or be roused out of their sleep. (Job 14:10–12)

As mentioned above, throughout most of the Old Testament there is no hope of an afterlife (2 Sam 14:14 cited above; Job 7:9; 10:21–22; 14:10–12; Pss 6:5; 30:9; 39:13–14; 88:4–5, 11–13; 104:29 [cf. Gen 2:7]; 115:17; Prov 2:18–19). First Chronicles 29:15 says, "Our days on the earth are like a shadow, and there is no hope." Instead, death leads only to the grave (Ps 89:48; Isa 38:18; Ezek 28:8; 31:14). For example: "For the fate of humans and the fate of animals is the same; as one dies, so dies the other. They all have the same breath, and humans have no advantage over the animals; for all is vanity. All go to one place; all are from the dust, and all turn to dust again" (Eccl 3:19–20). Later in the same book it says,

> But whoever is joined with all the living has hope, for a living dog is better than a dead lion. The living know that they will die, but the dead know nothing; they have no more reward, and even the memory of them is lost. Their love and their hate and their envy have already perished; never again will they have any share in all that happens under the sun. (Eccl 9:4–6)

There are flashes of hope such as in the Book of Isaiah (53:10–12), which says that the Servant of Yahweh would be apportioned a lot with the great, and therefore triumph over death.[30] Still another passage from Isaiah (25:8) says that the LORD of hosts will "destroy death forever" (NABRE). Finally, some point to Isaiah 26:19 as expressing the existence of life after death, but the Hebrew of that verse is problematic. Where there is clarity about the afterlife from Isaiah is this passage:

> For Sheol cannot thank you,
>   death cannot praise you;
> those who go down to the Pit cannot hope
>   for your faithfulness. (Isa 38:18)

This idea is echoed in Psalm 6:5: "For in death there is no remembrance of you; in Sheol who can give you praise?" And yet, there are some psalms that wrestle with the afterlife. Two psalms in particular (49:15; 73:24–28) express hope that

Yahweh will deliver the author from death, but what that deliverance looks like is unclear.[31]

Even the New Testament expresses the fleeting nature of life:

> Come now, you who say, "Today or tomorrow we will go to such and such a town and spend a year there, doing business and making money." Yet you do not even know what tomorrow will bring. What is your life? For you are a mist that appears for a little while and then vanishes. (Jas 4:13–14)

Those familiar with the New Testament might be surprised to read those words from the Letter of James. We are a "mist" (some translations, e.g., the NABRE, use "puff of smoke") that appears for a little while and then vanishes. This passage echoes many others in the Old Testament such as Psalm 37:20, which says, people "like smoke they vanish away"; Psalm 39:5, which says every person "stands as a mere breath"; Psalm 62:9, "they are together lighter than a breath"; Psalm 144:4, "[human beings] are like a breath; their days are like a passing shadow"; or Job 7:16, "for my days are a breath." There are others too, but the point is made. The Bible recognizes the fragility and even shortness of human life. When we couple that insight with the recognition that most of the Bible expresses no hope of life after death, we begin to see how profound that hope really is.

From the latter half of the first century BCE, the deuterocanonical 2 Maccabees, written in Greek, speaks of a resurrection to life. This book, not found in most Protestant Bibles, is itself a condensation of a larger five-volume work (2 Macc 2:23), which extols the virtue and justice of obeying God's law (the Torah) amid suffering and death. Those who suffer and die for God's law are promised life, to be raised up by the God for whose laws they gave their lives (2 Macc 2:17–18). As for those who caused the suffering and death of the just, the God of justice will see to it that they are punished in the next life, even if they seem to prosper in this life. Thus, the God of justice will not be undermined. Justice will be meted out, if not in this life, in a life to come.

The postulation of an afterlife wherein God metes out justice is a theological development in the scriptures, as the late composition of 2 Maccabees might indicate. For a people who did not see or believe in an afterlife, that idea was postulated to account for the lack of perceived justice in the earthly realm. So even if it does not appear that the just are rewarded and the wicked suffer in this life, one could be assured that God would exact justice in the end. For, as it says in another late, deutero-canonical book written in Greek, "Righteousness is undying" (Wis 1:15; NABRE).

In a few Old Testament cases we find a belief or hope that the just will live with God; that is to say, those who died faithful to God will be rewarded by being raised up to be with him forever. Their death is not their end. This set the stage for the New Testament understanding of what happened to Jesus after his death. In an act of ultimate justice, God had raised Jesus from the dead, exalted him to his own right hand, glorified him, and lifted him up into heaven. Rather than see these as independent different actions, they are better understood as different ways of speaking of ultimately the same fundamental statement of faith: Jesus lives now eternally with God. The execution of Jesus was overturned by God himself, who lifts up the righteous.

In the face of loss, especially death, people of faith turn to God. But what about those who do not have faith? The avowed atheist, writer, and public intellectual Christopher Hitchens (1949–2011) was diagnosed with esophageal cancer and died eighteen months later at the age of sixty-two. He had spent much of his career as a writer dismissing religious thought, so when his diagnosis was made public, there was a mixture of reaction. Some believers encouraged him to make amends with God, whereas other believers maintained this was some sort of divine judgment. Still many other believers offered prayers for him. Hitchens himself maintained his atheism and wondered what the prayers were for, his health or his conversion. He said plainly that if his body overcame the cancer and that the religious had claimed it had been due to their prayers, that would have been "irritating."[32] He died as he had lived—an avowed atheist.

Another popular atheist who passed away expressed a meaningful life in this way, which is simply gratitude:

> The world is so exquisite, with so much love and moral depth, that there is no reason to deceive ourselves with pretty stories for which there's little good evidence. Far better, it seems to me, in our vulnerability, is to look Death in the eye and be grateful every day for the brief but magnificent opportunity that life provides.[33]

An "attitude of gratitude" can be shared by believers as well as atheists, and there might be something that believers could learn from such a display. Rather than looking forward to a life eternal, this transitory life on earth is worthy of thanks and celebration. Though Hitchens and Sagan died as atheists, there are others who become believers just as some believers lose faith and become atheists, or at least agnostic.

The modern author and memoirist Amber Scorah writes about losing her faith as a Jehovah's Witness. Her new life in New York is splendid, especially with her new baby boy. But tragically, when she first left him at daycare at four months old, he died, a parent's nightmare. She says, "Death without hope also makes one acutely grateful for life, sensitive to it." Though friends and loved ones reached out to comfort her, their words did not console. In Amber's own words, "But though they were sincere, none of what they said was true. There is no heaven, no door at the end of my life that I will find my boy behind, no paradise Earth. He simply had ceased to exist." She continues, "If belief were a choice, I might choose it. But it's not. I don't trade in certainty anymore. If there is something more, it's not something we know. If we can't even grasp how it is that we got here, how can we know with any certainty where, if anywhere, we go when we die?" She concludes by saying, "I will never know who my child would have been, but I know his love. If there is a God, this is what he gave me."[34]

Ms. Scorah is only one example of thousands of people who, without faith in God, have made meaning of death, and therefore life. In broad strokes, she captures what is a recurring theme, that of appreciation and gratitude for the time we do have on this earth with loved ones. It's possible to recognize the fleeting nature of life and try to not take it for granted. Too often, only when someone is gone, dead, or euphemistically "passed away" do we take stock of our relationship(s). But we do not need to wait until it is too late to be appreciative and grateful. Paradoxically, that is one thing unbelievers may "teach" people of faith, for whom it may be too flippant to say that the departed loved one is in a "better place" where we will meet again someday.

CONCLUSION

I've grown up. I don't believe in father figures
anymore, like God, Kennedy or Hitler. I'm no
longer searching for a guru. I'm no longer
searching for anything. There is no search.
There's no way to go. There's nothing. This is it.

—John Lennon, 1967 (*Anthology*, 357)

There is nothing better for mortals than to
eat and drink, and find enjoyment in their
toil. This also, I saw, is from the hand of God.

—Eccl 2:24

This book started with the popular but elusive topic of
"God's Plan" and some of the ways it's been used throughout history. Some comedians have had interesting takes on
the topic as well. In the brief run of the television show
Arrested Development,[1] there is a scene where Michael (played by
Jason Bateman) unexpectedly meets his son, George Michael
(played by Michael Cera), in the hallway of an apartment
building and an awkward conversation ensues, due in part to
their being interested in the same girl, named Rebel. Michael
tells his son that he cannot join him because he has plans. His
son says he has plans too. The conversation begins and ends
with references to the divine.

SIGNS, SUPERSTITIONS, AND GOD'S PLAN

Michael: You got plans, huh? Well, we make plans, and God laughs.

George Michael: That's right.

M: Right?

GM: No, I always want to make plans, but...

M Hmm.

GM: You don't want to be laughed at.

M: Tell me. Yeah. Well, I won't laugh. Do you have plans with Rebel?

GM: Uh, yeah, I do, yeah. I do. Yeah, no.

M: Good for you guys.

GM: No, it's–it's fun stuff, yeah. Stuff I think, even if you weren't God, you'd find funny.

M: You can't ask for more than that. But that's none of my business, yeah? Only reason I ask, 'cause I'm going on a scuba trip. Um, yeah, came back in town to get my gear. Only reason I'm here, um, you know. It's a last-minute thing. Several weeks at sea. You'd hate it.

GM: Yeah, not my thing.

M: I shouldn't have even asked you.

GM: Oh, did you ask?

M: Ah...I don't want to inter-....You shouldn't cancel your plans with Rebel, you know. Rain check.

GM: Uh, it's tomorrow or...?

M: Hmm? We leave today.

GM: Ah.

M: So, yeah. God's probably....I can almost hear him laughing, you know? Although, maybe, I imagine, it doesn't make him laugh anymore.

GM: I mean, so much of life is, uh, plans. It would just be the same joke over and over.

M: So he's....It's not funny anymore.

GM: What's he laughing at?

Comedians cut to the quick. Likely we have all heard the saying referenced above: "Make plans and God laughs." Our plans often do come to naught and may seem risible in the eyes of God. And yet, as the writers note, what is God laughing at? Thwarted plans would be the same joke over and over. The idea that God laughs at our plans is a harmless popular anecdote, reminding us that our plans are often unfulfilled. Even so, we can find meaning and happiness despite apparent setbacks.

A "DO-OVER"

In the game of chess, especially with computers, it is easy to go back in the game and replay it from a certain point. Rather than move a knight at a critical point in the game, I can instead move a rook and see how the game unfolds. This kind of replaying and analysis often makes a better chess player, as one learns the ins and outs of the game, becoming more familiar with the board, the interaction of the pieces, and anticipated countermoves.

But in life there are no replays. There are no "take backs." We only move forward. If someone chooses a technical school rather than an entry-level job, or one college as opposed to another, or pursues biology rather than history, or dates this person rather than that person, or moves from one town or city to another, or chooses to focus on a career rather than a family, we cannot go back for a "do-over" to see what might have happened otherwise. And this is to say nothing about the countless other daily and pedestrian actions we choose throughout our lives, such as what we eat, the means and way we go to work, or who we might encounter in a passing exchange. Even more, many factors in our lives are determined by forces outside our control including when and where we are born, who our parents are, how much they participate in our raising, whether they divorce, whether we move, or whether or how tragedy might strike. Life is not like the movies *Sliding Doors* or *Back to the Future*. We make the best decisions we can at the time, due to factors controlled and uncontrolled and reasons known and unknown. We can never know what might have been. There is no going back for a do-over.

The Swedish poet and psychologist Tomas Tranströmer expresses this sensation in *The Blue House*. A happy man views his eighty-year-old home from a different vantage point in the woods and contemplates what might have been. "It is always so early in here, before the crossroads, before the irrevocable choices. Thank you for this life! Still, I miss the alternatives. The sketches, all of them, want to become real." The "solution" is to posit that these other lives based on other choices are unfolding elsewhere: "Without really knowing, we divine; our life has a sister ship, following quite another route."[2]

BEING LED OR BEING HELD BACK?

Each of our decisions, from major and minor down to the quotidian, make us who we are. There are good choices and those that seemed good at the time. There are choices to which we give a great deal of thought and others that seem inconsequential. With the benefit of hindsight, we can see more clearly how one decision opened a pathway that led to another, and then to more. In a passage reminiscent of the role of conscience, it is said that Socrates claimed, "There is some divine influence, *daimonion* he called it, which I always obey, though it never urges me on, but often holds me back."[3] Some, like Socrates, experience being held back; others may experience a sense of being guided, as the narrator says in Wendell Berry's novel *Jayber Crow*.

> If you could do it, I suppose, it would be a good idea to live your life in a straight line—starting, say, in the Dark Wood of Error, and proceeding by logical steps through Hell and Purgatory and into Heaven. Or you could take the King's Highway past appropriately named dangers, toils, and snares, and finally cross the River of Death and enter the Celestial City. But that is not the way I have done it, so far. I am a pilgrim, but my pilgrimage has been wandering and unmarked. Often what has looked like a straight line to me has been a circle or a doubling back. I have been in the Dark Wood of Error any number of times. I have known something of Hell, Purgatory, and Heaven, but not always in that order. The names of many snares and dangers have been made known to me, but I have seen them only in looking back. Often I have not known where I was going until I was already there. I have had my share of desires and goals, but my life has come to me or I have gone to it mainly by way of mistakes and surprises. Often I have received better than I have deserved. Often my fairest hopes have rested on bad mistakes. I am an ignorant pilgrim, crossing a dark valley. And yet

for a long time, looking back, I have been unable to shake off the feeling that I have been led—make of that what you will.[4]

Though the character in the novel has the feeling of being led, we might suggest that his looking back to perceive his being led could be "confirmation bias." From a more rational, less romantic, and perhaps more detached point of view, we could say that any path we chose would bring us to a point where we could look back and believe or even sense that we had been led. We would have the sense that somehow the universe had worked out for us, even if we faced tragedy. And we could make this affirmative statement even recognizing that background forces and environments beyond our control were at work.

But even this point of view is from our immediate personal story. If we expand the scope of view further still to include our parents, their parents, or even their parents' parents, we can see that our own individual presence here at all is a remarkable and inestimable product of chance, dependent upon millions and millions of still more chance events. Ultimately, each individual human being happened by chance, and it is up to us to create our own destiny and fashion meaning for ourselves.

Theologically speaking, such a point of view is certainly compatible with a belief in God. The individual human being recognizes the precariousness of his or her own existence and attributes it to God's gift, freely given. The parable of the talents comes to mind, wherein Jesus tells a story about someone who entrusted his servants with sums of money while he was away (Matt 25:14–30; cf. Luke 19:11–27). Upon his return he asked what these servants did with the money. According to Matthew's version of the story, the first two doubled theirs, but the third hid the money. The first two were praised and entrusted with more while the third servant was chastised. One moral of the story might be that human beings are to grow the gifts and talents they have, but not according to a predetermined (or divine) plan. Growth rather than stagnancy is the goal.

Furthermore, we might consider how disrespectful or even theologically arrogant it sounds for any human being to claim to know God's will, or to claim that events happened in accord with some divine plan. For a believer, it would certainly be more accurate and humbling to admit, like the Apostle Paul, that the ways of God are "inscrutable" (Rom 11:33), or as the prophet Isaiah says,

> For my thoughts are not your thoughts,
>   nor are your ways my ways, says the LORD.
> For as the heavens are higher than the earth,
>   so are my ways higher than your ways,
>   and my thoughts than your thoughts.
>   (Isa 55:8–9)

Thus, whether one is a believer or not, it is possible to appreciate the wonder of life, the miracle of our own personal existence, to be grateful, and to make of our life what we can. With gratitude for the limited time we have, we can discern meaning in the midst of it all. A line from Ecclesiastes opened this chapter, extolling the goodness of physical delights, that they are from the hand of God. Later in the same book, the biblical author develops that theme:

> Go, eat your bread with enjoyment, and drink your wine with a merry heart; for God has long ago approved what you do....Enjoy life with the wife whom you love, all the days of your vain[5] life that are given you under the sun, because that is your portion in life and in your toil at which you toil

under the sun. Whatever your hand finds to do, do with your might; for there is no work or thought or knowledge or wisdom in Sheol, to which you are going. (Eccl 9:7–10)

The reader is exhorted to enjoy this life with a partner, and enjoy food and drink throughout all one's days. From the author's viewpoint, there is no afterlife. In the face of that stark reality, we should enjoy all the days of our limited life. The Book of Ecclesiastes makes this point multiple times (e.g., 3:12–13; 5:17).

Meaning is not "out there," something extrinsic and objective to be grasped. Instead, as Frankl posited, each of us creates meaning for ourselves. Meaning is internal and subjective even if many of the categories we use for meaning—religion, superstition, providence, "it was meant to be," and so on—are shared widely. In fact, religious identity is one way of making meaning that might work for some but does not necessarily for others, even those in the same family.

When we investigate the past, even the past of our own lives, we can see patterns or reasons why matters took a certain course. We might even discern cause and effect. After pondering the past, it is not difficult to imagine that "things happen for a reason" or for a believer, "God had a plan." In this way, we are constructing meaning from the events of the past. The believer layers onto the events of the past a theological construct, God's plan. In this way we might say that human beings, then, are the ones who construct God's plan, much like Luke used the term in his own Gospel and in Acts to speak of what God had done in Jesus. We are the ones who say what is or is not God's plan; not every claim that something is God's plan makes it so. We are also the ones to say whether something happened for a reason or is due to providence or fate. We construct meaning for ourselves.

132

Both the believer and nonbeliever can find themselves in a similar place. Kate Bowler wrote, "Plans are made. Plans come apart. New delights or tragedies pop up in their place. And nothing human or divine will map out this life, this life that has been more painful than I could have imagined, more beautiful than I could have imagined."[6] The astronomer Carl Sagan wrote, as we read earlier,

> The world is so exquisite, with so much love and moral depth, that there is no reason to deceive ourselves with pretty stories for which there's little good evidence. Far better, it seems to me, in our vulnerability, is to look Death in the eye and be grateful every day for the brief but magnificent opportunity that life provides.[7]

EPILOGUE

Perhaps our place in the world is easier to see when we look not at ourselves, but at others, or even other species. Let us take the spotlight we have been shining on ourselves and focus it elsewhere. When we consider the number of living mammals on the earth (to say nothing of all living creatures), we call to mind that each mammalian species has a highly active brain and each cares for and nurses their young. If we could ask various mammals and they could respond, they might think that they were meant to be here, that all of creation was intended for them. For example, a dolphin perfectly suited to its environment, raising its young, who were each "meant to be," might consider itself in a unique position. But there are thousands upon thousands of dolphins born each year. Is each meant to be? Or do we as humans freely admit that evolutionary forces are at work in small and subtle ways, shaping each new baby dolphin. We know that thousands of dolphins are born each year, but is each one intended as that particular one by some benevolent deity(ies)? Is each the result of providential oversight or care? Or if these dolphins were not conceived and born, would it simply be that others would have been conceived and born? We can imagine this thought experiment with every living creature on the earth, and not only those here now, but over millennia, as life continues, evolves, and adapts to its environment. Every living thing, including each of us, is a product of evolution. In short, "evolution by natural selection is the acid that burns through every myth about ordained purposes and meanings."[1]

The naturalist E. O. Wilson states the insight eloquently: "Each human being, with no exception, belongs to a single, reproductively isolated species of animal confined by its idiosyncratic biology and social behavior. Before this characterization can be read as a hint of divine interpretation, be aware that the same can be said of hundreds of other social species, from siphonophore jellyfish and web-spinning communal spiders to fellow mammals like porpoises and wolves."[2]

> Human existence may be simpler than we thought. There is no predestination, no unfathomed mystery of life. Demons and gods do not vie for our allegiance. Instead, we are self-made, independent, alone, and fragile, a biological species adapted to live in a biological world. What counts for long-term survival is intelligent self-understanding, based upon a greater independence of thought than that tolerated today even in our most advanced democratic societies.[3]

A story about Albert Einstein might also serve to illustrate the point further. Einstein received a letter in 1950 from a rabbi who had lost one of his two daughters. The rabbi wanted advice from Einstein about what words to offer his now only daughter (and perhaps the same words might also console him, the father). Einstein replied with the following letter:

> A human being is part of the whole, called by us "Universe," a part limited in time and space. He experiences himself, his thoughts and feelings, as something separated from the rest, a kind of optical delusion of his consciousness. This delusion is a

kind of prison for us, restricting us to our personal desires and to affection for a few persons nearest to us. Our task must be to free ourselves from this prison by widening our circle of compassion to embrace all living creatures and the whole of nature in its beauty. Nobody is able to achieve this completely, but the striving for such achievement is in itself a part of the liberation and foundation for inner security.[4]

It is not known whether these words comforted or consoled the remaining daughter or her father. But they reflect Einstein's insight that we, human beings, all creatures, and all of nature, are part of the same whole that we call the universe. When we expand our horizon to recognize this, our inner lives may become both more free and more secure.

E. O. Wilson says something similar when he notes that "we alone among all species have grasped the reality of the living world, seen the beauty of nature, and given value to the individual. We alone have measured the quality of mercy among our own kind. Might we now extend the same concern to the living world that gave us birth?"[5]

Wilson, the naturalist who coined the term *biodiversity*, goes further with his insight in stating, "We have created a Star Wars civilization, with Stone Age emotions, medieval institutions, and godlike technology. We thrash about. We are terribly confused by the mere fact of our existence, and a danger to ourselves and to the rest of life."[6] Even if earlier generations believed that an all-powerful God would not allow a species to be wiped off the face of the earth, we now recognize that we, the human species, is the cause of a drastic destruction of and permanent elimination of thousands of species so that there is now considered to be a Sixth Extinction.[7]

As we create systems of meaning making for ourselves,

it would be wise to expand our horizon to include all living things, all of nature, the entire known universe, and then contemplate our own limited role. This insight articulated especially well by those considered atheist or agnostic can provide rich fruit for contemplation by the believer.

NOTES

PREFACE

1. CNN, "Falwell Apologizes to Gays, Feminists, Lesbians," September 14, 2001, http://edition.cnn.com/2001/US/09/14/Falwell.apology/.

2. CNN, "Falwell Apologizes."

3. CNN, "Falwell Apologizes." According to CNN, Pat Robertson said, "We have sinned against Almighty God, at the highest level of our government, we've stuck our finger in your eye. The Supreme Court has insulted you over and over again, Lord. They've taken your Bible away from the schools. They've forbidden little children to pray. They've taken the knowledge of God as best they can, and organizations have come into court to take the knowledge of God out of the public square of America."

4. Andrew Kaczynski and Nathan McDermott, "Senate Candidate Roy Moore This Year Suggested 9/11 Might Have Been Punishment for US Turning Away from God," CNN, September 14, 2017, http://www.cnn.com/2017/09/14/politics/kfile-roy-moore-9-11/index.html.

5. Fox News, "Justice with Judge Jeanine," accessed March 16, 2021, https://www.facebook.com/judgejeaninepirro/videos/764480387414844/.

6. Samuel Butler, based on public domain edition, revised by Timothy Power and Gregory Nagy, 1900. Homer *Odyssey*, 1.1–20, accessed March 16, 2021, http://www.perseus.tufts.edu/hopper/text?doc=Perseus:text:1999.01.0136.

7. Elizabeth Dias, "Meet the Pastor Who Prays with Donald Trump," *Time*, September 14, 2016, http://time.com/4493530/donald-trump-prayer/.

8. Frank Bailey with Ken Morris and Jeanne Devon, *Blind Allegiance to Sarah Palin: A Memoir of Our Tumultuous Years* (New York: Howard Books, 2011), 328.

9. Ben Smith and Andy Barr, "Ex-Aide's Book a Harsh Palin Portrait," *Politico*, February 22, 2011, https://www.politico.com/story/2011/02/ex-aides-book-a-harsh-palin-portrait-049938.

An early draft of the manuscript of Frank Bailey's book was leaked to the press and seems to have included portions that did not make it into the final published version. The line "Plus, I had nothing to wear, and God knew that too" seems to have succumbed to the editor's pen as it is not in the published book.

10. Most of us have heard of Donner as the name of Santa's reindeer: Donar and Blitzen (thunder and lightning).

11. Cicero, *De Divinatione*, II.18.7, in *Cicero: De Senectute De Amicitia De Divinatione*, ed. and trans. William Armistead Falconer (Cambridge, MA: Harvard University Press, 1923), http://www.perseus.tufts.edu/hopper/text?doc=Perseus%3Atext%3A2007.01.0043%3Abook%3D2%3Asection%3D18.

12. Flavius Josephus, *The Wars of the Jews or History of the Destruction of Jerusalem*, Project Gutenberg Ebook, trans. William Whiston, 3.387–92, http://www.gutenberg.org/files/2850/2850-h/2850-h.htm.

CHAPTER ONE

1. Accessed March 16, 2021, https://www.facebook.com/ChristianMingle/posts/845555252156936.

2. Paul Farhi, "Evoking God Has Been Good for Christian Mingle," *Washington Post*, January 8, 2013, https://www.washingtonpost.com/lifestyle/style/evoking-god-has-been-good-to-christianmingle/2013/01/09/c3f28148-59dd-11e2-9fa9-5fbdc9530eb9_story.html?utm_term=.0d5ee0bac4b8.

3. John Pavlovitz, "Why God May Want You to Leave Your Marriage," blog, July 28, 2016, accessed September 20, 2021,

https://johnpavlovitz.com/2016/07/28/why-god-may-want-you-to-leave-your-marriage/.

4. Elton Yutzy, *God's Plan for Man and Planet Earth: From the "Big Bang" to the New Heaven and Earth* (Bloominton, IN: Westbow Press, 2013), 6–8.

5. Antony Beevor, *Ardennes 1944: Battle of the Bulge* (New York: Viking, 2015), 277.

6. Beevor, *Ardennes 1944*, 284.

7. Beevor, *Ardennes 1944*, 287.

8. Abraham Lincoln, Washington, DC, September 2, 1862?, in *Collected Works of Abraham Lincoln*, vol. 5, accessed March 16, 2021, https://quod.lib.umich.edu/l/lincoln/lincoln5/1:893?rgn=div1;view=fulltext.

9. Francis B. Carpenter, *Six Months at the White House* (New York: Hurd and Houghton, 1866), 282.

10. Associated Press, "Palin: Iraq War 'A Task That Is from God,'" *The Oklahoman*, September 4, 2008, https://www.oklahoman.com/article/3292633/palin-iraq-war-a-task-that-is-from-god.

11. Ben Wedeman, "The War against ISIS Was All a Waste," CNN, October 14, 2019, https://www.cnn.com/2019/10/14/middleeast/isis-battle-wasted-gains-intl/index.html.

12. For example, Pope Leo XIII, *Testem Benevolentiae Nostrae* (Concerning New Opinions, Virtue, Nature and Grace, with Regard to Americanism) (1899).

13. Daniel Burke, "Does God Really Want Donald Trump to Be President?" CNN, February 1, 2019, https://edition.cnn.com/2019/02/01/us/sanders-trump-god/index.html.

14. Michael W. Chapman, "Rev. Franklin Graham to CNN: God Put Trump in the Presidency," *CNS News Blog*, January 26, 2018, https://www.cnsnews.com/blog/michael-w-chapman/rev-graham-cnn-trump-president-reason-god-put-him-there.

15. Jason LeMiere, "Scott Pruitt Told Donald Trump He Is President Because of 'God's Providence' in Resignation Letter," *Newsweek*, July 7, 2018, http://www.newsweek.com/scott-pruitt-donald-trump-god-1010529.

16. McKay Coppins, "God's Plan for Mike Pence," *The Atlantic* (January/February 2018), https://www.theatlantic.com/magazine/archive/2018/01/gods-plan-for-mike-pence/546569/.

17. Erik Gorski, "Palin Says Election Rests in God's Hands," AP/*Denver Post*, October 22, 2008, https://www.denverpost.com/2008/10/22/palin-says-election-result-rests-in-gods-hands-2/.

18. Daniel Burke, "Rick Perry Says Trump (and Obama) Were 'Ordained by God' to Be President," CNN, November 25, 2019, https://www.cnn.com/2019/11/25/politics/rick-perry-donald-trump-god/index.html.

19. Julie Gallagher, "Pompeo Agrees It's Possible God Raised Trump to Protect Israel from Iranian Aggression," CNN, March 23, 2019, https://www.cnn.com/2019/03/22/politics/mike-pompeo-donald-trump-israel-golan-heights/index.html.

20. Peter Montgomery, "Sarah Palin Says She'll Run for Senate If God Wants Her To, Christians Do More to Support Her," Right Wing Watch: A Project of People for the American Way, July 30, 2021, https://www.rightwingwatch.org/post/sarah-palin-says-shell-run-for-senate-if-god-wants-her-to-christians-do-more-to-support-her/.

21. See *The Axe Files with David Axelrod*, episode 283, November 12, 2018, https://www.cnn.com/audio/podcasts/axe-files?episodeguid=gid://art19-episode-locator/V0/4pjkWGaWxAioFiyEVLHsl1WK6bs0sgzXyQI6P6mTnIg.

22. Amy Gardner and David Weigel, "Liberal Challenger Defeats Conservative Incumbent in Wisconsin Supreme Court Race," *Washington Post*, April 14, 2020, https://www.washingtonpost.com/politics/liberal-challenger-defeats-conservative-incumbent-in-wisconsin-supreme-court-race/2020/04/13/7d1195ec-7d9e-11ea-8013-1b6da0e4a2b7_story.html.

23. *Collected Works of Abraham Lincoln*, vol. 8, 332–33, https://quod.lib.umich.edu/l/lincoln/lincoln8/1:711?rgn=div1;singlegenre=All;sort=occur;subview=detail;type=boolean;view=fulltext;q1=with+malice+toward+none.

24. See the recent Vatican document from the Congregation on Catholic Education, "'Male and Female He Created Them': Towards a Path of Dialogue on the Question of Gender in Education" (Feb-

ruary 2, 2019), which takes its title from Genesis 1:26, https://www
.vatican.va/roman_curia/congregations/ccatheduc/documents/
rc_con_ccatheduc_doc_20190202_maschio-e-femmina_en.pdf. The
document reiterates that "Holy Scripture reveals the wisdom of the
Creator's design" in making humanity male and female, or at least
reflecting masculinity and femininity (no. 32).

25. Adam Kelsey and John Verhovek, "NC Congressional
Candidate Once Questioned Whether Careers Were 'Healthiest Pur-
suit' for Women: Mark Harris, a Former Pastor, Urged Women to
Understand Their 'Core Calling,'" *ABC News*, July 5, 2018, https://
abcnews.go.com/Politics/nc-congressional-candidate-questioned
-careers-healthiest-pursuit-women/story?id=56342956.

26. Sharon Otterman, "Cardinals on Opposite Sides of the
Hudson Reflect Two Paths of Catholicism," *New York Times*, July 16,
2017, https://www.nytimes.com/2017/07/16/nyregion/cardinals
-catholicism-same-sex-attraction-gay.html.

27. Only those under the age of eighty are eligible to vote in a
conclave, the meeting that elects the pope. The number of the elector-
cardinals is limited to 120, though, in actuality, from time to time that
cap is exceeded.

28. Otterman, "Cardinals on Opposite Sides of the Hudson
Reflect Two Paths of Catholicism."

29. For example, John Henry Hopkins, "A Scriptural, Eccle-
siastical, and Historical View of Slavery," in *From the Days of the
Patriarch Abraham, to the Nineteenth Century. Addressed to the Right Rev.
Alonzo Potter* (New York: Pooley & Co., 1864).

30. Chris Massie and Andrew Kaczynski, "Trump Judicial
Nominee Said Transgender Children Are Part of 'Satan's Plan,'
Defended 'Conversion Therapy,'" CNN, September 20, 2017, http://
www.cnn.com/2017/09/20/politics/kfile-jeff-mateer-lgbt-remarks/
index.html.

31. Diogenes Laertius, *Lives*, 6.2.59.

32. Pliny the Elder, *Natural History*, 2.5.

33. The Greek term *logismon* is used only twice in the New Testament, each by Paul, to mean "thought" or "argument/speculation"
(Rom 2:15; 2 Cor 10:5).

34. A scriptural antidote to the prosperity gospel is found in 1 Timothy 6:6–11, a passage rarely cited by such preachers.

35. Other translations, e.g., NABRE, use "plan" here.

36. My translation from the Italian. Pontifical Biblical Commission, *The Interpretation of the Bible in the Church*, April 15, 1993, 35: "Il metodo storico-critico è il metodo indispensabile per lo studio scientifico del significato dei testi antichi," https://www.vatican.va/roman_curia/congregations/cfaith/pcb_documents/rc_con_cfaith_doc_19930415_interpretazione_it.html.

37. Joseph A. Fitzmyer, *The Gospel According to Luke*, 2 vols. (Garden City, NY: Doubleday, 1982), 1:179.

38. Irenaeus, a second-century theologian who merged biblical ideas with a Greek philosophical system, speaks of God's plan as all of creation for the sake of the incarnation (e.g., *Adversus Haereses* 4.38.3). Melito of Sardis, another second-century theologian, preached an Easter homily in which he claims (italics mine):

> Indeed, the Lord *prearranged* his own sufferings in the patriarchs, and in the prophets, and in the whole people of God, giving his sanction to them through the law and the prophets. For that which was to exist in a new and grandiose fashion was *pre-planned* long in advance, in order that when it should come into existence one might attain to faith, just because it had been predicted long in advance. (*Peri Pascha*, 57)

39. This brief section, beginning with the subhead Bible, is based on an earlier article I wrote, "Luke as the Master Architect of 'God's Plan': An Analysis of a Distinctive Lucan Concept," *Biblical Theology Bulletin* 50, no. 4 (November 2020): 227–35.

40. United States Conference of Catholic Bishops, *United States Catholic Catechism for Adults* (Washington, DC: USCCB Publishing, 2006). See also United States Conference of Catholic Bishops, *United States Catholic Catechism for Adults*, 2nd ed. (Washington, DC: USCCB Publishing, 2019).

41. Rick Warren, "God's Plan for your Pain," Devotional Blog, September 18, 2020, https://pastorrick.com/gods-plan-for-your-pain-2/.

42. Rick Warren, "God's Plan to Bring You to Heaven," Devotional Blog, November 6, 2020, https://pastorrick.com/gods-plan-to-bring-you-to-heaven-3/.

43. Rick Warren, "God's Plan for You Started Before You Were Born," Devotional Blog, May 30, 2017, https://www.crosswalk.com/devotionals/daily-hope-with-rick-warren/daily-hope-with-rick-warren-may-30-2017.html.

44. Many popular theological or religious "purpose-driven" books today will cite the passage from Jeremiah, "Before I formed you in the womb I knew you" (Jer 1:5), to claim that each person has a unique role or plan to fulfill.

CHAPTER TWO

1. Strabo, *Geography*, 13.4.14.

2. Pliny the Elder, *Natural History*, 2.95.

3. H. Pfanz, G. Yüce, A. H. Gulbay, et al., "Deadly CO_2 Gases in the Plutonium of Hierapolis (Denizli, Turkey)," *Archaeological and Anthropological Sciences* 11 (2019): 1359–71, https://doi.org/10.1007/s12520-018-0599-5.

4. Plato, *Republic*, 10.11 §§612e–13a, in Plato, *Republic, Volume II: Books 6–10*, ed. and trans. Christopher Emlyn-Jones and William Preddy, Loeb Classical Library 276 (Cambridge, MA: Harvard University Press, 2013), 461.

5. Dionysius of Halicarnassus, *Roman Antiquities* 5.7.1, 54.1; 10.10.2; 15:3.1; 20.9.2; see also 2.26.3.

6. Flavius Josephus, *The Wars of the Jews or History of the Destruction of Jerusalem*, Project Gutenberg Ebook, trans. William Whiston, 7.315; 7.8.5, http://www.gutenberg.org/files/2850/2850-h/2850-h.htm.

7. See also Pss 136:25, 104:27–28.

8. See manuscript evidence from P46; A, B, 81 in Eberhard Nestle, Erwin Nestle, Barbara Aland, Kurt Aland, Iōan. D. Karavidopoulos, Carlo Maria Martini, Bruce M. Metzger, and Holger Strutwolf. 2012. *Novum Testamentum Graece.*

9. "V. The Declaration of Independence as Adopted by Congress, 11 June–4 July 1776," *Founders Online*, National Archives,

https://founders.archives.gov/documents/Jefferson/01-01-02-0176 -0006 (original source: *The Papers of Thomas Jefferson*, vol. 1, *1760– 1776*, ed. Julian P. Boyd [Princeton: Princeton University Press, 1950], 429–33).

10. Allen Jayne, *Jefferson's Declaration of Independence: Origins, Philosophy, and Theology* (Lexington: The University Press of Kentucky, 2015).

11. "III. First Inaugural Address, 4 March 1801," *Founders Online*, National Archives, https://founders.archives.gov/documents/Jefferson/01-33-02-0116-0004 (original source: *The Papers of Thomas Jefferson*, vol. 33, *17 February–30 April 1801*, ed. Barbara B. Oberg [Princeton: Princeton University Press, 2006], 148–52).

12. Manifest Destiny was the nineteenth-century belief that the United States was destined to expand westward throughout North America.

13. "Second Inaugural Address, 4 March 1805," *Founders Online*, National Archives, https://founders.archives.gov/documents/Jefferson/99-01-02-1302.

14. Ron Chernow, *Grant* (New York: Penguin, 2017), 343.

15. Lincoln's Second Inaugural, U.S. National Archives, accessed March 16, 2021, https://www.ourdocuments.gov/doc.php?doc=38.

16. John Toland, *Adolf Hitler*, First Anchor Books edition (New York: Doubleday, 1976), 388.

17. See Toland, *Hitler*, 389.

18. Toland, *Hitler*, 403.

19. Toland, *Hitler*, 591.

20. Toland, *Hitler*, 433–34.

21. Toland, *Hitler*, 594.

22. Toland, *Hitler*, 689.

23. Toland, *Hitler*, 693.

24. Toland, *Hitler*, 811.

25. Toland, *Hitler*, 796–99.

26. Toland, *Hitler*, 813–14.

27. Toland, *Hitler*, 812–13.

28. Toland, *Hitler*, 592–93.

29. Toland, *Hitler*, 737–38.
30. Toland, *Hitler*, 790.

CHAPTER THREE

1. The movie is based on the short story by Philip K. Dick, "Adjustment Team," *Orbit Science Fiction* 4 (September–October 1954): 81–100.

2. Fate, as seen in the story of Hitler's surviving the 1944 assassination attempt, is often associated with Providence.

3. John Toland, *Adolf Hitler*, First Anchor Books edition (New York: Doubleday, 1976), 802.

4. Toland, *Hitler*, 799.

5. Toland, *Hitler*, 591.

6. OCD, s.v. "fate."

7. Flavius Josephus, *The Antiquities of the Jews*, Project Gutenberg Ebook, trans. William Whiston, 16.397 [16.11.8], https://www.gutenberg.org/files/2848/2848-h/2848-h.htm.

8. Chernow, *Grant*, 597.

9. Winston Churchill, *The Gathering Storm*, vol. 1, *The Second World War* (Boston: Houghton Mifflin, 1948), 667.

10. Joseph Fontenrose, *The Delphic Oracle: Its Responses and Operations with a Catalogue of Responses* (Berkeley: University of California Press, 1978).

11. Strabo, *Geography*, 9.3.5. See also Euripides, IA, 760–61.

12. Herodotus, *The Histories*, ed. A. D. Godley (Cambridge, MA: Harvard University Press, 1920), 1.47.1, http://www.perseus.tufts.edu/hopper/text?doc=Perseus%3Atext%3A1999.01.0126%3Abook%3D1%3Achapter%3D47.

13. Herodotus, *The Histories*, 1.47.3.

14. Herodotus, *The Histories*, 1.48.2.

15. Herodotus, *The Histories*, 1.53.3, http://www.perseus.tufts.edu/hopper/text?doc=Hdt.+1.53&fromdoc=Perseus%3Atext%3A1999.01.0126.

16. Herodotus, *The Histories*, 7.140, http://www.perseus.tufts.edu/hopper/text?doc=Hdt.%207.140&lang=original.

17. Herodotus, *The Histories*, 7.141, http://www.perseus.tufts.edu/hopper/text?doc=Perseus%3Atext%3A1999.01.0126%3Abook%3D7%3Achapter%3D141.

18. Plato, Apology 21b, in *Plato in Twelve Volumes*, vol. 1, trans. Harold North Fowler, intro. W. R. M. Lamb (Cambridge, MA: Harvard University Press, 1966), http://www.perseus.tufts.edu/hopper/text?doc=Perseus%3Atext%3A1999.01.0170%3Atext%3DApol.%3Asection%3D21b.

19. Plato, *Apology* 21a–d.

20. Plato, *Apology* 21d, in *Plato in Twelve Volumes*, http://www.perseus.tufts.edu/hopper/text?doc=Perseus%3Atext%3A1999.01.0170%3Atext%3DApol.%3Asection%3D21d.

21. Plutarch, *Life of Alexander*, 1.14.6–7.

22. Polybius, *Hist.* 10.2.11. Cicero too speaks of divination, prophecy, and oracles in *De Divinatione*, I.18.34.

CHAPTER FOUR

1. Dionysius, *Roman Antiquities*, 10.2.5.

2. *Merriam-Webster.com Dictionary*, s.v. "omen," accessed March 27, 2021, https://www.merriam-webster.com/dictionary/omen.

3. J. D. Vance, *Hillbilly Elegy: A Memoir of a Family and Culture in Crisis* (New York: Harper, 2016), 95.

4. Robert Boling, *Judges*, 1st ed., Anchor Bible 6A (New York: Doubleday, 1975), 141.

5. See S. Tolkowsky, *Journal of the Palestine Oriental Society* 3 (1923): 197–99.

6. Sarah Weathers Burton, "Putting Out the Fleece," updated October 21, 2015, https://www.bjupress.com/resources/articles/t2t/putting-out-the-fleece.php.

7. Denis Coday, "US Cardinal Asserts Unity with Pope after Former Doctrine Chief Questions Francis," *National Catholic Reporter*, November 2, 2017, https://www.ncronline.org/news/vatican/us-cardinal-asserts-unity-pope-after-former-doctrine-chief-questions-francis?utm_source=NOV_2_weinandy&utm_campaign=cc_110217&utm_medium=email.

8. Carl E. Olson, "Fr. Thomas G. Weinandy Explains His Critical Letter to Pope Francis," *The Catholic World Report*, November 1, 2017, https://www.catholicworldreport.com/2017/11/01/fr-thomas-g-weinandy-explains-his-critical-letter-to-pope-francis/.

9. John Toland, *Adolf Hitler*, First Anchor Books edition (New York: Doubleday, 1976), 299.

10. Plutarch, *Life of Alexander*, 14.5, in *Plutarch's Lives*, English trans. Bernadotte Perrin (Cambridge, MA: Harvard University Press, 1919), 7, http://www.perseus.tufts.edu/hopper/text?doc=Plut.+Alex.+14.5&fromdoc=Perseus%3Atext%3A1999.01.0243.

11. Cicero, *De Divinatione*, II.43.19, in *Cicero: De Senectute De Amicitia De Divinatione*, ed. and trans. William Armistead Falconer (Cambridge, MA: Harvard University Press, 1923), http://www.perseus.tufts.edu/hopper/text?doc=Cic.+Div.+2.43&fromdoc=Perseus%3Atext%3A2007.01.0043.

12. Suetonius, *Julius Caesar*, 81.1–3, LCL edition, 1913–1914, trans. J. C. Rolfe, http://penelope.uchicago.edu/Thayer/e/roman/texts/suetonius/12caesars/julius*.html.

13. Dio, *Roman History*, 44.17.1–3, LCL edition, 1916, http://penelope.uchicago.edu/Thayer/E/Roman/Texts/Cassius_Dio/44*.html.

14. Suetonius, *Augustus*, 94.11, LCL edition, 1913, https://penelope.uchicago.edu/Thayer/E/Roman/Texts/Suetonius/12Caesars/Augustus*.html.

15. Cicero, *De Divinatione*, I.77.35, http://www.perseus.tufts.edu/hopper/text?doc=Cic.+Div.+1.77.

16. Cicero, *De Divinatione*, II.8.21, http://www.perseus.tufts.edu/hopper/text?doc=Perseus%3Atext%3A2007.01.0043%3Abook%3D2%3Asection%3D21.

17. Toland, *Hitler*, 414.

18. Albert Speer, *Inside the Third Reich* (New York: Simon & Schuster, 1970), 162, https://archive.org/details/insidethirdreich00albe/page/162/mode/2up.

19. Suetonius, *Augustus*, 95.1.

20. Cicero, *De Natura Deorum*, 2.3.

21. "As for him, he was warned of the plot in advance by soothsayers and was warned also by dreams. For the night before he

was slain his wife dreamed that their house had fallen in ruins and that her husband had been wounded by some men and had taken refuge in her bosom; and Caesar dreamed he was raised aloft upon the clouds and grasped the hand of Jupiter." Dio, *Roman History* 44.17.1–3.

22. Suetonius, *Julius Caesar*, 81.3.

23. Suetonius, *Augustus*, 94.4.

24. Suetonius, *Augustus*.

25. See *Anchor Bible Dictionary*, 1st ed. (1992), s.vv. "Dreams in the New Testament" and "Greco-Roman Literature," 2.231.

26. Toland, *Hitler*, 708.

27. Faith Karimi, "Woman Was Worried before Her Plane Crashed in Iran, Her Husband Says. She Called Him 20 Minutes before Takeoff," CNN, January 9, 2020, https://www.cnn.com/2020/01/09/middleeast/iran-plane-crash-victim-husband-speaks/index.html.

28. Martin Luther King, "I See the Promised Land," in *A Testament of Hope: The Essential Writings of Martin Luther King, Jr.*, ed. James Melvin Washington (San Francisco: Harper & Row, 1986), 279–86.

CHAPTER FIVE

1. See Ulla Koch-Westenholz, *Mesopotamian Astrology: An Introduction to Babylonian and Assyrian Celestial Divination* (Copenhagen: Carsten Niebuhr Institute of Near Eastern Studies, 1995).

2. Virgil, *Aeneid*, 2.694.

3. Suetonius, *Julius Caesar*, 88.1, LCL edition, 1913–1914, trans. J. C. Rolfe, http://penelope.uchicago.edu/Thayer/e/roman/texts/suetonius/12caesars/julius*.html.

4. Raymond E. Brown, *The Birth of Messiah: A Commentary on the Infancy Narratives in Matthew and Luke* (Garden City, NY: Doubleday, 1977), 170–173. Brown reviews many possibilities of what this "star" might have been, including a supernova, a comet, or even a planetary conjunction.

5. Suetonius, *Nero*, 36.

6. Pliny the Elder, *Natural History*, 2.30; see also Plutarch, *Caesar*, 69.4; Flavius Josephus, *The Antiquities of the Jews*, Project

Gutenberg Ebook, trans. William Whiston, 14.12.3, https://www
.gutenberg.org/files/2848/2848-h/2848-h.htm.

7. Thucydides, *History of the Peloponnesian War*, Book 7.23,
trans. Richard Crawley, http://classics.mit.edu/Thucydides/pelop
war.7.seventh.html.

8. Samuel Eliot Morison, *Christopher Columbus, Mariner* (Boston: Little, Brown, 1955), 184–92.

9. "60 Minutes/Vanity Fair: Superstition," *CBS News*, February 2, 2015, https://www.cbsnews.com/news/60-minutesvanity-fair
-superstition.

10. Claire Gecewicz, "'New Age' Beliefs Common among
Both Religious and Nonreligious Americans," *Pew Research Center*,
October 1, 2018, https://www.pewresearch.org/fact-tank/2018/10/
01/new-age-beliefs-common-among-both-religious-and-nonreligious
-americans/.

11. *Cosmos: A Personal Voyage*, episode 3, "Traveller's Tales,"
directed by Adrian Malone, written by Carl Sagan, Ann Druyan, and
Steven Soter, presented by Carl Sagan, aired October 26, 1980, on
PBS.

12. John Toland, *Adolf Hitler*, First Anchor Books edition
(New York: Doubleday, 1976), 590.

13. Toland, *Hitler*, 624.

14. See George Stein, *Hitler* (Englewood Cliffs, NJ: Prentice
Hall, 1968), 83–87.

15. Shelby Grad and David Colker, "Nancy Reagan Turned
to Astrology in White House to Protect Her Husband," *Los Angeles Times*, March 6, 2016, https://www.latimes.com/local/lanow/la
-me-ln-nancy-reagan-astrology-20160306-story.html.

16. Joan Quigley, *What Does Joan Say? My Seven Years as White
House Astrologer to Nancy and Ronald Reagan* (New York: Birch Lane
Press, 1990).

17. Jack Hitt, "Inside the Secret Sting Operations to Expose
Celebrity Psychics," *New York Times Magazine*, February 26, 2019,
https://www.nytimes.com/2019/02/26/magazine/psychics
-skeptics-facebook.html?smprod=nytcore-ipad&smid=nytcore-ipad
-share.

18. Carols Baeza, dir., *The Simpsons*, season 5, episode 9, "The Last Temptation of Homer," aired December 9, 1993, on Fox.

19. "Severe Weather 101: Frequently Asked Questions About Lightning," The National Severe Storms Laboratory, accessed March 3, 2022, https://www.nssl.noaa.gov/education/svrwx101/lightning/faq/.

20. For a good scientific treatment of lightning, see Martin A. Uman, *The Lightning Discharge* (Mineola, NY: Dover, 2001). Uman opens with mythological stories of lightning from antiquity and the Middle Ages.

21. Suetonius, *Augustus*, 94.2.

22. Toland, *Hitler*, 575.

23. Maureen Cleave, "On a Hill in Surrey...A Young Man, Famous, Loaded, and Waiting for Something," *London Evening Standard*, March 4, 1966, 10.

24. "Lightning Hits KLUE," *Longview Morning Journal* 34, no. 194 (August 14, 1966): A2.

25. "Lightning Strikes St Peter's Basilica as Pope Resigns," *BBC News*, February 12, 2013, http://www.bbc.com/news/av/world-europe-21421810/lightning-strikes-st-peter-s-basilica-as-pope-resigns.

26. Pliny the Younger, *Letters*, 6.16; 5.20.

27. Pliny the Younger, *Letters*, 6.16.

28. Dionysius of Halicarnassus, *The Roman Antiquities*, 10.2.2.

29. "Vatican Condemns Catholic Radio That Said Quakes Were God's Wrath for Gay Law," *Reuters News Service*, November 4, 2016, https://news.trust.org/item/20161104190930-g5l9e/.

30. *American Experience: FDR*, part 4, "The Juggler (1940–1945)," written and directed by David Grubin, aired October 12, 1994, on PBS.

CHAPTER SIX

1. *Merriam-Webster.com Dictionary*, s.v. "superstition," accessed March 27, 2021, https://www.merriam-webster.com/dictionary/superstition.

2. The stories and legends behind these superstitious beliefs are fascinating. For example, knocking on wood is said to have originated with people knocking on trees to summon spirits to protect them from evil. Crossing one's fingers is said to go back to early Christians who made the sign of the cross with their fingers to protect themselves from evil or danger. Tossing salt over one's shoulder comes from antiquity when salt was precious and valuable. Spilling it was thought to be a bad omen.

3. "60 Minutes/Vanity Fair: Superstition," *60 Minutes*, February 2, 2015, https://www.cbsnews.com/news/60-minutesvanity-fair-superstition.

4. See Julia Buttree and E. T. Seton, *The Rhythm of the Redman: In Song, Dance, and Decoration* (New York: A. S. Barnes & Co., 1930).

5. Antony Beevor, *Ardennes 1944: Battle of the Bulge* (New York: Viking, 2015), 101.

6. Beevor, *Ardennes 1944*, 245.

7. Zosimus, *New History* 4.18.

8. Jacobus de Voragine (archbishop of Genoa, 1275), *The Golden Legend; or Lives of the Saints*, ed. F. S. Ellis, Temple Classics (1st ed. 1483; English ed. 1483 by William Caxton) (Hammersmith: Kelmscott Press, 1900, reprinted 1922, 1931), https://sourcebooks.fordham.edu/basis/goldenlegend/GoldenLegend-Volume3.asp.

9. See *The Procession of Saint Gregory in the Basilica of Saint Peter in Chains*; and Jacopo Zucchi, *The Procession of St. Gregory* (1573–75), oil on wood panel at the Pinacoteca Vaticana, Rome, et al.

10. Michelle Krupa, "As Hurricane Season Starts, Coastal Catholics Call on This Holy Go-Between for Protection from Devastating Storms," CNN, June 1, 2019, https://www.cnn.com/2019/06/01/us/hurricane-season-our-lady-of-prompt-succor-trnd/index.html.

11. Other names for Mary or Marian apparitions throughout the world include the following: Our Lady of Guadalupe, Our Lady of Victory, Queen of Heaven, Star of the Sea, Mother of Mercy, Our Lady of Loreto, Our Lady of La Salette, Our Lady of Fatima, Our Lady of Lourdes, Our Lady of La Vang, Our Lady of Zeitoun, and even Our Lady of Good Help in Green Bay, Wisconsin.

12. Jeffrey Gettleman, Hari Kumar, and Kai Schultz, "A Man's Last Letter before Being Killed on a Forbidden Island," *New York Times*, November 23, 2018, https://www.nytimes.com/2018/11/23/world/asia/andaman-missionary-john-chau.html.

CHAPTER SEVEN

1. *A Late Show with Stephen Colbert*, August 25, 2020. During the pandemic, the Colbert show was called *A Late Show*.... When he's in the Ed Sullivan Theater it's *The Late Show*... (as I understand it).

2. Wisdom literature is a broad category, but the following biblical books are often placed here: Job, Psalms (some, not all), Proverbs, Ecclesiastes, Song of Songs, Wisdom, and Sirach. Many of these works were written later, closer to the New Testament than the Torah, and they reflect in many ways a deep reflection on the human condition.

3. Titus Livius, *Early History of Rome*, 5.51.5., in Livy, *Books V, VI and VII*, with an Engl. trans. (Cambridge, MA: Harvard University Press, 1924), http://www.perseus.tufts.edu/hopper/text?doc=Perseus%3Atext%3A1999.02.0154%3Abook%3D5%3Achapter%3D51.

4. Leah Asmelash and Jeanne Bonner, "Karma Caught Up to This Ketchup Thief. Now, Heinz Is Helping the Thief Out," CNN, August 10, 2019, https://www.cnn.com/2019/08/10/us/heinz-ketchup-thief-restaurant-trnd/index.html.

5. *Oxford Dictionary*, s.v. "serendipity," accessed March 27, 2021, https://www.lexico.com/en/definition/serendipity.

6. Tim Riley, *Lennon: The Man, The Myth, The Legend—the Definitive Life* (New York: Hyperion, 2011), 18–22.

7. Walter Everett, *The Beatles as Musicians: Revolver through the Anthology* (New York: Oxford University Press, 1999), 200–201.

8. "60 Minutes/Vanity Fair: Superstition," *60 Minutes*, February 2, 2015, https://www.cbsnews.com/news/60-minutesvanity-fair-superstition.

9. Viktor E. Frankl, *Man's Search for Meaning* (Boston: Beacon Press, 2006).

10. Frankl, *Man's Search*, 150.

CHAPTER EIGHT

1. According to a 1991 survey by the Library of Congress and the Book of the Month Club. See Esther B. Fein, "Book Notes," *New York Times*, November 20, 1991, https://www.nytimes.com/1991/11/20/books/book-notes-059091.html.

2. Viktor E. Frankl, *Man's Search for Meaning* (Boston: Beacon Press, 2006), 99. Italics in the original.

3. "His survival was a combined result of his will to live, his instinct for self-preservation, some generous acts of human decency, and shrewdness; of course, it also depended on blind luck, such as where he happened to be imprisoned, the whims of the guards, and arbitrary decisions about where to line up and who to trust or believe. However, something more was needed to overcome the deprivations and degradations of the camps. Frankl drew constantly upon human capacities such as inborn optimism, humor, psychological detachment, brief moments of solitude, inner freedom, and a steely resolve not to commit suicide" (William J. Winslade, "Afterword," in Frankl, *Man's Search*, 158).

4. Richard Dawkins, *The God Delusion* (Boston: Houghton Mifflin, 2006), 360.

5. Daniel J. Siegel, *Mindsight: The New Science of Personal Transformation* (New York: Bantam, 2010), 259.

6. Frankl, *Man's Search*, 109.

7. Frankl, *Man's Search*, 120–21.

8. "Dutch Fertility Doctor Used Own Sperm to Father 49 Children, DNA Tests Show," BBC, April 12, 2019, https://www.bbc.com/news/world-europe-47907847#:~:text=A%20Dutch%20fertility%20doctor%20accused,clinic%20in%20Bijdorp%2C%20near%20Rotterdam. See also Sarah Zhang, "The Fertility Doctor's Secret: Donald Cline Must Have Thought No One Would Ever Know. Then DNA Testing Came Along." *The Atlantic*, April 2019, https://www.theatlantic.com/magazine/archive/2019/04/fertility-doctor-donald-cline-secret-children/583249/.

9. Libby Copeland, "Who Was She? A DNA Test Only Opened New Mysteries: How Alice Collins Plebuch's Foray into

'Recreational Genomics' Upended a Family Tree," *Washington Post*, July 27, 2017, https://www.washingtonpost.com/graphics/2017/lifestyle/she-thought-she-was-irish-until-a-dna-test-opened -a-100-year-old-mystery/?hpid=hp_hp-top-table-main_dna-blurb %3Ahomepage%2Fstory&utm_term=.acfae36e533f.

10. According to the Gospel of Matthew (1:3–6), Jesus himself had at least four unusual links in his genealogy. Tamar, Rahab, Ruth, and Bathsheba, the wife of Uriah, bore sons in circumstances that were unusual and even scandalous. For example, according to Genesis 38, Tamar was the daughter-in-law of Judah. She was twice widowed when Judah took her as a prostitute without recognizing her and impregnated her. When it became known that she was pregnant and without a husband, Judah was willing to put her to death. But Tamar's own cunning saved her as she was able to prove it was Judah himself who impregnated her.

11. *Froward* means someone difficult to deal with, contrary.

12. "You" refers to "Homunculus," which is a reference to an older belief that each spermatozoan was a small, but complete human.

13. Christiaan Huygens, *De Ratiociniis in Ludo Aleae* (Ex officinia J. Elsevirii, 1657).

14. David Hand, *The Improbability Principle: Why Coincidences, Miracles, and Rare Events Happen Every Day* (New York: Scientific American/Farrar, Straus and Giroux, 2014), 27. Cf. Joseph Mazur, *Fluke: The Math and Myth of Coincidence* (New York: Basic Books, 2016).

15. Siegel, *Mindsight*, 238.

16. Peter Brugger and Kirsten I. Taylor, "ESP: Extrasensory Perception or Effect of Subjective Probability?" *Journal of Consciousness Studies* 10, nos. 6–7 (2003): 221–46.

17. David Williams, "Man Wins $1 Million Lottery with the Numbers His Family Has Played for 50 Years," CNN, August 21, 2020, https://www.cnn.com/2020/08/21/world/lottery-lucky-numbers -50-trnd/index.html.

18. Francis Bacon, *The New Organon: Or True Directions Concerning the Interpretation of Nature* (1620) Aphorisms, Book One XLVI (as quoted in Hand, *The Improbability Principle*, 158).

19. Paul Rosenfeld, John G. Kennedy, and Robert A. Giacalone, "Decision Making: A Demonstration of the Postdecision Dissonance Effect," *The Journal of Social Psychology* 126, no. 5 (1986): 663–65, https://doi.org/10.1080/00224545.1986.9713640.

20. Carl Sagan, *Billions and Billions* (New York: Random House, 1997), 214.

21. For example, Kashmira Gander, "What Happens When You Die? Scientists Have Re-created a Near-Death Experience to Find Out What It Feels Like," *Newsweek*, September 4, 2018, https://www.newsweek.com/what-happens-when-you-die-scientists-have-recreated-near-death-experience-1102292?spMailingID=4059235&spUserID=MzQ4OTU3NTY4NDAS1&spJobID=1110199935&spReportId=MTExMDE5OTkzNQS2. Sam Parnia, MD, *Erasing Death: The Science That Is Rewriting the Boundaries Between Life and Death* (New York: Harper One, 2013).

22. "Near-death experiences (NDEs) are complex subjective experiences, which have been previously associated with the psychedelic experience and more specifically with the experience induced by the potent serotonergic, *N,N-Dimethyltryptamine* (DMT). Potential similarities between both subjective states have been noted previously, including the subjective feeling of transcending one's body and entering an alternative realm, perceiving and communicating with sentient 'entities' and themes related to death and dying." "DMT Models the Near-Death Experience," *Frontiers in Psychology*, August 15, 2018, https://www.frontiersin.org/articles/10.3389/fpsyg.2018.01424/full. See also, Rick Strassman, *DMT: The Spirit Molecule—A Doctor's Revolutionary Research into the Biology of Near-Death and Mystical Experiences* (Rochester, VT: Park Street Press, 2000).

23. Griff Witte and Chelsea Janes, "The Coronavirus Was Spreading. The Parties Went On. Now Comes the Pain," *Washington Post*, April 9, 2020, https://www.washingtonpost.com/national/the-coronavirus-was-spreading-the-parties-went-on-now-comes-the-pain/2020/04/09/39bdbe1e-7908-11ea-a130-df573469f094_story.html.

24. See Job 7:6, "My days are swifter than a weaver's shuttle, and come to their end without hope."

25. See also Bart D. Ehrman, *Heaven and Hell: A History of the Afterlife* (New York: Simon & Schuster, 2020); Alan F. Segal, *Life after Death: A History of the Afterlife in the Religions of the West* (New York: Doubleday, 2004), see esp. 150–52 for Job, "in my flesh I shall see God"; Keith Hopkins, *Death and Renewal* (Cambridge: Cambridge University Press, 1983).

26. See Ezek 18; 22:31; 33:10–20; Sir 17:23; Joel 3:4; Jer 23:19.

27. See also Exod 20:5; 34:7; Deut 5:9; Jer 32:18.

28. Deut 24:16; Jer 31:29–30; Ezek 18:2–4.

29. For example, not long after the outbreak of COVID-19 in early 2020, Cardinal Raymond Burke attributed the breakout of the disease to sin. "There is no question that great evils like pestilence are an effect of original sin and of our actual sins. God, in His justice, must repair the disorder which sin introduces into our lives and into our world." He also called on priests to continue saying Mass (despite the social isolation and quarantines recommended by public health experts), claiming, "We cannot simply accept the determinations of secular governments, which would treat the worship of God in the same manner as going to a restaurant or to an athletic contest." Claire Giangravé, "Catholic Cardinal Burke Says Faithful Should Attend Mass Despite Coronavirus," *Religion News Service*, March 21, 2020, https://religionnews.com/2020/03/21/catholic-cardinal-burke-says-faithful-should-attend-mass-despite-coronavirus/.

30. Joseph A Fitzmyer, Raymond Edward Brown, and Roland Edmund Murphy, eds., *The New Jerome Biblical Commentary* (Hoboken, NJ: Prentice-Hall, 1990), 1314.

31. Brian Schmisek, *Resurrection of the Flesh or Resurrection from the Dead* (Collegeville, MN: Liturgical Press, 2013), 49–92.

32. Christopher Hitchens, *Mortality* (New York: Grand Central Publishing, 2012).

33. Carl Sagan, *Billions and Billions* (New York: Random House, 1997), 215.

34. Amber Scorah, "Surviving the Death of My Son after the Death of My Faith: I Had Lost the One Thing That Could Have

Numbed My Pain," *New York Times*, May 31, 2019, https://www
.nytimes.com/2019/05/31/opinion/sunday/life-after-death.html.

CONCLUSION

1. Troy Miller, dir., *Arrested Development*, season 5, episode 3, "Everyone Gets Atrophy," aired May 29, 2018, on Netflix.

2. Tomas Tranströmer, "The Blue House," in *The Great Enigma: New Collected Poems*, trans. Robin Fulton (New York: New Directions, 2006), 169.

3. Cicero, *De Divinatione*, I.122.54, in *Cicero: De Senectute, De Amicitia, De Divinatione*, ed. and trans. William Armistead Falconer (Cambridge, MA: Harvard University Press, 1923), http://www
.perseus.tufts.edu/hopper/text?doc=Perseus%3Atext%3A2007.01
.0043%3Abook%3D1%3Asection%3D122.

4. Wendell Berry, *Jayber Crow: The Life Story of Jayber Crow, Barber, of the Port William Membership, as Written by Himself* (Washington, DC: Counterpoint Press, 2000), 79 (opening of chap. 12).

5. Some translations (e.g., New International Version) use the word *meaningless* here rather than *vain*.

6. Kate Bowler, *Everything Happens for a Reason and Other Lies I've Loved* (New York: Random House, 2018), 161.

7. Carl Sagan, *Billions and Billions* (New York: Random House, 1997), 215.

EPILOGUE

1. E. O. Wilson, quoting Daniel Dennet in *Origins of Creativity* (London: Penguin, 2018), 93.

2. Wilson, *Origins of Creativity*, 86.

3. E. O. Wilson, *The Meaning of Human Existence* (New York: Liveright Publishing, 2014), 26.

4. Einstein letter quoted in Daniel J. Siegel, *Mindsight: The New Science of Personal Transformation* (New York: Bantam, 2010), 255.

5. Wilson, *Meaning of Human Existence*, 132.

6. Edward O. Wilson, *The Social Conquest of Earth* (New York: Norton, 2012), 7.

7. Elizabeth Kolbert, *The Sixth Extinction: An Unnatural History* (New York: Henry Holt, 2014). Cf. Colin Barras, "How Humanity First Killed the Dodo, Then Lost It as Well," BBC Earth, April 9, 2016.

SUBJECT INDEX

SCRIPTURE INDEX

Scripture Index